THE HANDHELD ELECTRONIC GAME STORY

ANDREW MORTEN

AMBERLEY

ABOUT THE AUTHOR

Andrew Morten has had an interest in technology from an early age and went on to gain his degree in Electrical Engineering and Electronics from Coventry in 1987. His previous books include *Amstrads and Ataris: UK Home Computers in the 1980s, The Digital Watch Story* and *The Pocket Calculator Story.*

First published 2026

Amberley Publishing
The Hill, Stroud,
Gloucestershire, GL5 4EP

www.amberley-books.com

ISBN: 978 1 3981 3310 5 (print)
ISBN: 978 1 3981 3311 2 (ebook)

British Library Cataloguing in Publication Data.
A catalogue record for this book is available from the British Library.

Typeset in 10pt on 13pt Celeste.
Typesetting by SJmagic DESIGN SERVICES, India.
Printed in the UK.

Appointed GPSR EU Representative: Easy Access System Europe Oü, 16879218
Address: Mustamäe tee 50, 10621, Tallinn, Estonia
Contact Details: gpsr.requests@easproject.com, +358 40 500 3575

CONTENTS

INTRODUCTION

Video games have been with us in one form or another since the early 1970s, when machines started to appear in amusement arcades. The first arcade video games were space-themed, and two of the earliest were *Galaxy Game* and *Computer Space* in 1971.

Shortly after, video consoles for the home were released, the first of which was the *Magnavox Odyssey* in 1972. The twenty-eight built-in games were extremely basic, consisting of dots that could be moved around the screen via the hand controllers. The

Video games have their origin in arcade machines like these.

most popular game – a version of tennis – inspired Atari to bring out its arcade version: *Pong*. In this classic sports-themed game, a player moves an electronic bat up and down in order to bounce a ball around the screen. It was simple but also addictive. Players found that they wanted to play again and again to hone their skills and beat their high score, paving the way for a whole new form of leisure. But to play meant a trip to the arcades or taking over the family's TV set for an evening. What if these new games could be played anywhere?

Fortunately, the 1970s saw the start of a revolution in electronics. Advances in miniaturisation had led to the invention of the digital watch and the pocket calculator. On the back of these commercial successes, and using similar technology, the first portable electronic game – Mattel's *Auto Race* – went on sale in 1976. It was a simple driving game that used the red LEDs that were available at the time, but its simplicity was also its appeal. Its success paved the way for other manufacturers like Milton Bradley (MB), Entex and Bandai to enter the market with their own versions of handheld games.

With the development of the LCD screen, the consoles produced in the 1980s were more sophisticated, but also, thanks to smaller batteries, became truly pocket-sized. This was the beginning of a new market in consumer electronics. Though home computers had taken off in a big way at the same time, and game-playing had become one of their main uses (for example, the Sinclair Spectrum), pocket gaming found its own niche.

Initially launched in the Japanese home market, their popularity quickly spread to the US and the rest of the world. From the 1990s, the market was dominated by Nintendo's

One of the many Game Boy models.

hugely successful Game Boy, which was still a best seller over a decade later. Although aimed initially at children and young adults, where they could be played on the school bus, on car journeys or at break times, there was no real age barrier, and this was reflected in the sales figures. The number of Nintendo handheld consoles sold since the launch of the Game Boy is estimated at well over 500 million.

Even though today most people own a smartphone, and the number and variety of games available for those is bewildering, there is still a thriving handheld games market for those who want the best experience only a dedicated console can provide.

This book charts the rise of the portable electronic game from its beginnings, its development through leaps in technology, and the companies who were at the forefront of this gaming revolution.

1

BEGINNINGS

The 1970s amusement arcades got people hooked on video games, and fans didn't have to wait long to be able to own a miniature version of their favourite game – be it *Space Invaders* or *Pac-Man*.

The possibility of manufacturing electronic games that were portable required two things: the electronics had to be small enough to fit in a handheld case and a tiny display was needed that could show the gameplay.

The electronics revolution that started in the early 1970s had used the power of the newly invented microchip to give us the first digital watch in 1970 and the first pocket calculator

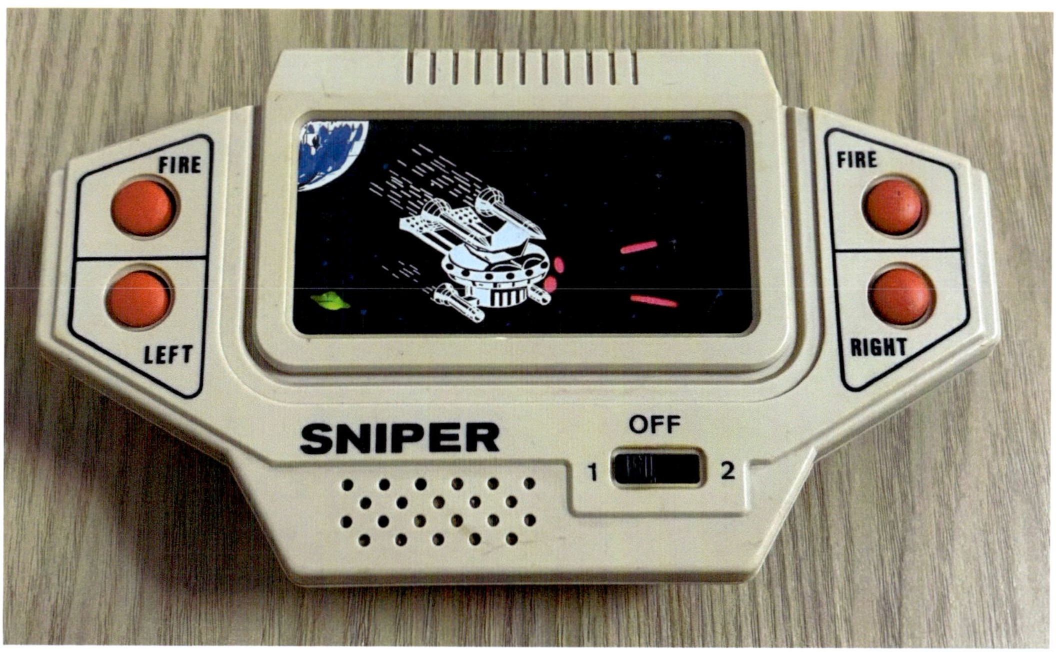

Sniper, an early LED space game.

in 1971. Further development of these devices, in particular the calculator, meant that by the middle of the decade they were the ideal starting point for a pocket gaming device. But the task of creating a display for even a simple game was challenging to say the least.

Both the first watch and calculator had used light-emitting diode (LED) displays to show numbers in red – the only technology available at the time. Although they were visible in most lighting conditions, their drawback was that they were power hungry and shortened battery life considerably. The big challenge was to develop these further into something on which a game could be played.

In the latter part of the 1970s, a more versatile display was being developed: the liquid-crystal display (LCD). Even though they were monochrome, they consumed a lot less power and so were a much more attractive alternative to the LED. In between the two technologies, a third type of display – the vacuum fluorescent display (VFD) – was developed and used in many pocket calculators of the mid-1970s. These work on a similar principle to fluorescent lighting tubes, where electric current passing through a gas causes it to glow. They were therefore adopted by games consoles as they were nice and bright and offered two different colours: red and blue-green. So, on the back of technology developed for the pocket calculator, manufacturers were now able to start producing simple handheld games with a choice of three different display types – LED, VFD or LCD.

The first generation of handheld games was characterised by being 'single-game'. That is, the games were hardwired into the consoles and didn't have swapable cartridges. These were on sale from 1976 until around 1983. Japan and the US were the leaders in the technology at the time and had the manufacturing plants already making calculator components. The market for handheld electronic games would quickly spread from these two countries and become truly global. For the first time, video game fans would be able to own portable versions of their favourite arcade games. This was both an exciting and competitive time for the fledgling handheld electronic games industry.

An early LCD game: *Hamburger Shop* by Bandai.

Mattel *Auto Race* (1976)

The first handheld electronic game – *Auto Race* – was launched by games and entertainment company Mattel in 1976. Mattel was founded in Los Angelos in 1945 by Harold 'Matt' Matson, Elliot Handler and his wife Ruth. Mattel are probably best known for the Barbie brand (created by Ruth Handler) and through acquisitions of household names like Tyco Toys, Corgi Toys and Fisher Price they became the world's leading toy maker until overtaken by Lego in 2018.

The idea for *Auto Race* came from Mattel engineer George J. Klose, who thought that a game could be created by modifying the hardware from a pocket calculator. Specifically, he thought that a basic racing car game could be created by animating individual display segments used in calculator displays. So, in 1974, Klose approached calculator chip manufacturer Rockwell to see if his vision was possible. Rockwell engineer Mark Lesser was given the job and set about modifying their B5000 chip to control the display and also a piezo-ceramic speaker to provide sound effects. The most difficult part was writing and then fitting the programming code for the game into the tiny amount of memory available – just 512 bytes! *Auto Race* was the first of what became known as first-generation consoles that played only a single game.

Auto Race went on sale in 1976 for $25, which made it an expensive item. The game measures 7.6 cm × 12.7 cm × 2.5 cm and has three controls and a small vertical display of the racetrack. There is a speaker behind the grille on the front and space in the rear for a 9V battery. Your car is represented by a red vertical dash at the bottom of the display and can be moved left or right using the button, with a car design below the display. Other cars

The first portable game: *Auto Race* by Mattel.

(also represented as dashes) move down from the top towards you and the aim is to move your car to avoid collision. There are four playing speeds, as set by the gear lever on the left. If you make it to the top of the screen in the four attempts given, the clock stops, giving you your score. If the clock reaches '99' it is game over.

The game was loosely based on racing car arcade games of the time in which the screen scrolled vertically, giving the impression of driving. Even though it was a simple game and the screen was small – hardly bigger than a calculator's display – it sold well enough for other similar games from Mattel. Their second and most popular release was *Football* in 1977, which also used a modified Rockwell chip and a three-line display of red LEDs, this time mounted horizontally. This was followed by *Soccer, Baseball* and *Hockey* in 1978. The same year also saw the release *of Battlestar Galactica Space Alert* based on the TV series. The object was to fire at enemies coming down the screen towards your ship – also represented by vertical red dashes – so not dissimilar to *Auto Race*!

Interestingly, Mattel re-released some of their games in 2001. The gameplay was exactly the same as the original but the display was updated to LCD. To annoy collectors (who like to keep their items in the original packaging), or perhaps unthinkingly, they came with batteries already installed, meaning they would have to be opened and removed or they would eventually corrode.

Mattel's *Battlestar Galactica Space Alert* game. (Courtesy of Joe Haupt, CC BY-SA 2.0)

Milton Bradley Microvision (1979)

The Milton Bradley Company, also known as 'MB', was founded in 1860 in Springfield, Massachusetts, and for the first 100 years predominantly made board games. During the American Civil War in 1861, MB created travel versions of checkers, chess and dominoes for bored soldiers to play. A century later, they produced *Twister*, the game that ties players up in knots on a mat, which had global success. In 1984, MB was bought by Hasbro and became Hasbro Gaming, but back in the 1970s MB had entered the electronic games market.

Their first electronic game, *Simon*, in 1978, comprised a circular console with red, yellow, blue and green sectors which lit up, and players had to compete in memorising sequences of colours and tones. It went on to become their best-selling game. A year later, in 1979, Mattel produced a world first: a console with swappable game cartridges, heralding the second generation of electronic games. Created by Jay Smith, the Microvision came with the game *Blockbuster* pre-installed. This was a handheld version of the arcade video game *Breakout* where players use a paddle to direct a ball onto a wall to knock out blocks. When it first went on sale in the US it cost $49.99 – expensive, but the Microvision's games were much more sophisticated than anything else available at the time.

The grey cartridge comprises the whole front of the console and contains a microprocessor with ROM space for the game and RAM for the player's score, along with the four control buttons and a window through which the screen can be viewed. The console itself contains an LCD screen and associated electronics, a circular control knob and a contact area that the buttons press upon.

The Microvision console with *Blockbuster*, Milton Bradley's version of *Breakout*.

Early versions of the game used an Intel 8021 processor and due to high power consumption, required two 9V batteries. Later versions used the Texas Instruments TMS1100 processors in the cartridges and these required only a single battery. It was marketed for ages eight to adult and, although described as a handheld games system, at 7.6 cm wide by 20.3 cm long, it was in no way pocket-sized!

The three buttons (left to right) set the number of balls per game, game speed and paddle size. The button below starts the game and the knob is turned left or right to move the paddle. Once a hole has been made in the wall, the ball can bounce behind and knock out blocks faster.

Once *Blockbuster* had been mastered, there were four other cartridges that could be purchased at the time: *Bowling, Shooting Star, Pinball* and *Connect 4*. A further seven games were released before the Microvision was discontinued in 1981.

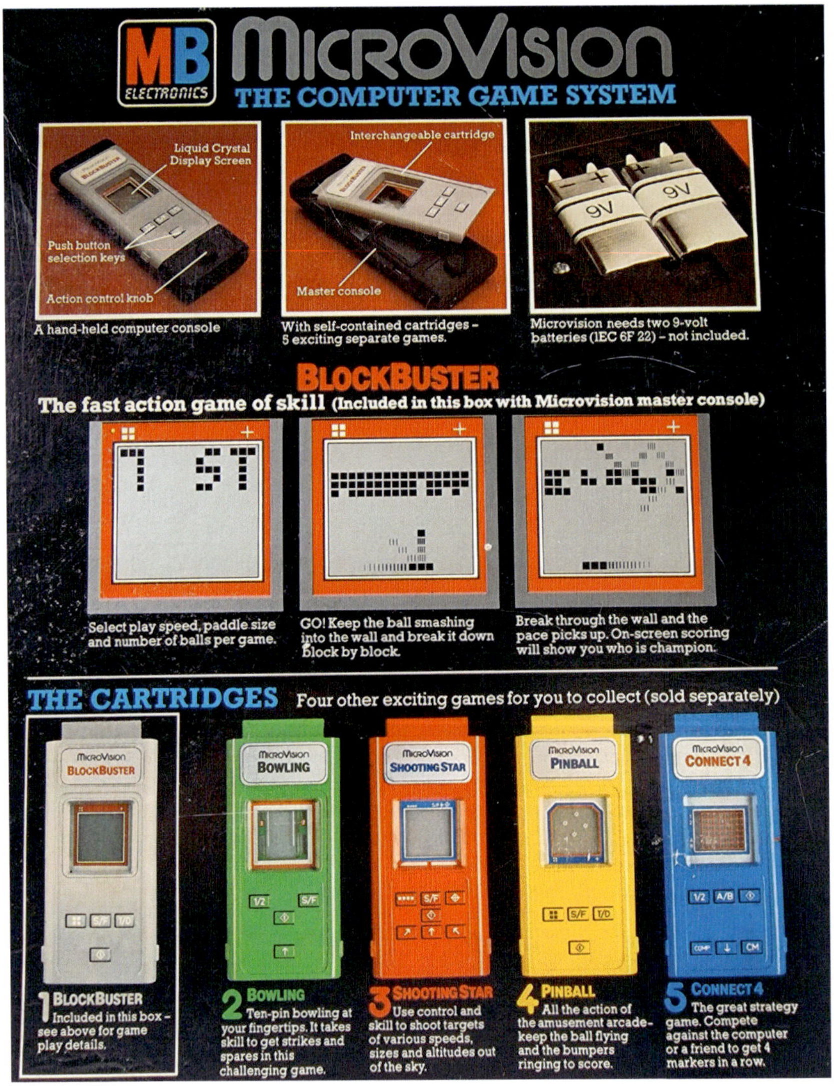

Instructions for use and the other games cartridges available.

Still working after forty-five years!

MB were an early adopter of LCD screen technology when other manufacturers were sticking with tried and tested LED. The Microvision screen with its 16 × 16 pixels worked well but over time could degrade and suffer leaks due to the early manufacturing processes. There is also a rubber membrane that the plastic keys press upon which will eventually stretch and thin, and the plastic buttons themselves can eventually break due to stressing of the plastic.

The Microvision is now a rare thing, and a working one rarer still, but occasionally can be seen on auction sites.

Bandai *Missile Invader* (1980)

The Bandai Company, which produced the *Missile Invader* game back in 1980, are the leading toy and entertainment company in Japan, but in the UK they are perhaps best known as the creators of the Tamagotchi craze in the 1990s. The strange egg-shaped pets were supposed to teach children how time-consuming it was to look after a real pet and are still sold today.

Bandai was formed in Tokyo in 1950 and initially produced toys for the home market. In the 1960s, they designed action figures to go with TV shows such as *Ultraman* and *Astro Boy* and also made electric *Thunderbird* vehicles. In the 1980s, their Bandai Electronics division released many electronic games for overseas markets, especially the US. In fact, there were at least 476 different models produced between 1980 and 1999. The titles were mostly either sports- or space-themed, or simplified versions of arcade games.

Initially, their games used LED displays, but from 1980 they also produced games with VFD (fluorescent) displays such as *Gunfighter* and *Grand Prix Champion*. From 1981

Bandai's *Missile Invader* game.

onwards Bandai started releasing games with LCD displays, such as *Juggling Seal,* though VFD display games were still released for a couple more years.

Missile Invader uses LEDs and is a version of the classic *Space Invaders,* first seen in the arcades in 1978. *Space Invaders* is part of a genre known as 'shoot 'em up' games, or STGs, where the player has a fixed gun and has to engage an enemy whilst being fired on themselves. The Bandai version is simplified in that there is just one invader at a time and scores you a point for hitting it, but as in the original game there is a UFO that moves along the top and scores 5 points for a hit. There are three control buttons: left and right for moving your missile station along the bottom and a 'fire' button on the side.

Inside, there is a single chip containing the game logic, a piezo-electric speaker for the sound effects, and just four passive electronic components, all powered by a 9V battery.

Bandai went on to create many overseas subsidiaries, including in the UK, where in the 1990s they developed games such as *Streetfighter II* for the Super Nintendo Entertainment System (SNES). In 2005, Bandai merged with Japanese game developer and amusement arcade operator Namco (creator of *Pac-Man*) to become Bandai Namco Holdings, the second-largest toy company in the world.

A Tamagotchi virtual pet from Bandai.

Entex Electronics *Space Invader* (1980)

In 1980, Entex Industries was a relative newcomer to the games market, having only been founded ten years earlier. It was set up in California by Nickolas Carlozzi, Nick Underhill and Englishman Tony Clowes, and the name comes from combining (N)ick and (T)ony with an X. They initially made model kits and also 'Loc Blocs', a direct competitor to Lego, but by 1980 their upmarket versions of arcade and sports games helped to achieve worldwide sales of $100 million. In the US, *Electronic Baseball 2* and a giant version of their pre-school Loc Blocs were voted best toys for Christmas 1979. Interestingly, their logo – an RAF roundel with a smiling face in the centre – came about because creator Ben Templeton thought that Tony Clowes seemed like an 'RAF type' and added the smiley, after getting permission from the RAF for the design.

In the original *Space Invader*, the aliens descend in waves whilst crabbing across the screen and releasing bombs onto your laser cannon. There are also buildings at the bottom of the screen which offer some protection. As the levels progress, the tension (and adrenalin!) rises because the more aliens you get rid of, the faster they descend. It's a game that requires total concentration and precise shooting to eliminate all the aliens from even just the first level. Its success spawned other STGs such as *Galaxians* and *Asteroids* in 1979.

This version of the game has the basics: aliens march to and fro across the screen dropping bombs on your base, whilst you shoot at them or hide behind one of the two shields. With the front of the case removed, the workings of the display are revealed. The screen comprises a grid of the game objects: your base positions at the bottom, aliens in the middle and saucers at the top. Behind each icon shape is an LED to light it up – forty-four in total – and when they are turned on and off in sequence it gives the illusion of movement. Simple! You can also see the contact pads for the three push switches (left, right and fire). The other two red slide switches are the on/off switch and the skill level (pro/amateur).

Left: *Space Invader* game by Entex.

Below: With the top removed, the LEDs for each of the alien positions are visible.

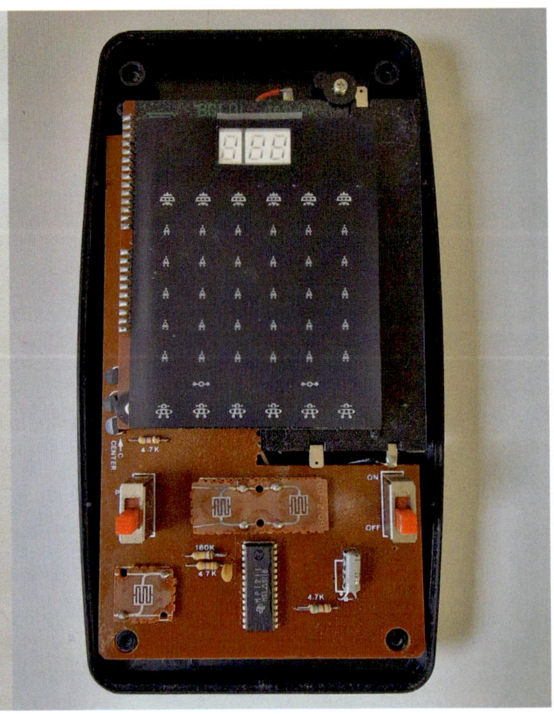

Entex *PacMan 2* (1980)

The year 1980 saw the release of one of the greatest ever video games: *Pac-Man*. It was created by Japanese games company Namco and was a departure from the more male-oriented sport and shoot 'em up-type games that had previously dominated the arcades.

Its designer – Toru Iwatani – wanted to create a game that was fun with cute characters and decided to base the game around eating. The name comes from the Japanese '*paku paku taberu*', meaning to open and close the mouth. The iconic Pac-Man character was born when Iwatani removed a slice from his salami pizza and saw a character with a mouth looking back at him!

Gameplay consists of moving Pac-Man through a maze to eat all the blue dots, thus completing the level. Periodically, four ghosts appear to try and catch you: Blinky (red), Pinky (Pink), Inky (cyan) and Clyde (orange). These each have different strategies to catch you and if they succeed you lose a life. To help you if cornered, you can exit via a tunnel on one side and be transported to the other side. Also, if you eat one of the power pills near the corners, the ghosts turn blue and run away. If you catch one, it's bonus points, and its eyes return back to the centre where it regenerates. In the arcade game there are 256 levels, and if all the bonus points were taken on every level it would give you a perfect score of 3,333,360.

Pac-Man has been awarded multiple accolades and records in its time, including 'Most Successful Coin-operated Game' from Guinness in 2008, with an estimated $14 billion revenue from all its franchises. It was transferred to the Atari 2600 home video console in

A screen from *Pac-Man*, the original video arcade game. (Courtesy of Namco)

The two-player Entex version of *Pac-Man*.

1982 and reproduced on most home computers of the 1980s such as the Commodore 64, VIC 20, Apple II and Spectrum.

This version by Entex is unusual in that it allows for either one or two players (hence *PacMan2*). With a single player, the number of ghosts chasing you is determined by the difficulty setting. With two players, one player controls Pac-Man whilst the other controls a ghost to chase you. There is also a demo mode. It has a nice, bright VFD display with the dots in red and the maze in blue, and with the four direction control buttons, it plays really well and gives a feel of the original arcade version.

CGL *Jet Fighters* (1982)

This *Jet Fighters* game from CGL (Computer Games Limited) is a variation on *Space Invaders* but with enemy planes shooting at you rather than aliens. You are armed with a missile launcher on the right-hand side of the screen which can be moved up and down using the lever in the top-right corner. The aim is to shoot down the jets (red) that come at you from the left with your missiles (green) to score points. There is also a battleship that appears occasionally on the left-hand side. It's quite good to play, and if you tilt the game 90 degrees you can see that it's just a more sophisticated version of *Auto Race*. The main

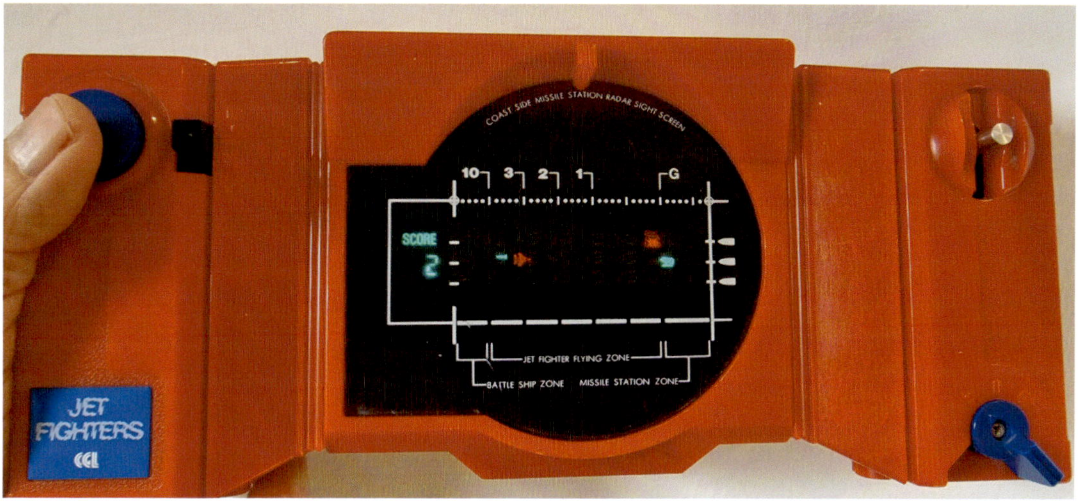

A game featuring fighter jets and missiles from CGL.

difference is that *Jet Fighters* uses a vacuum fluorescent display (VFD) rather than LEDs, which makes the display brighter and also allows the two colours, which is used here to distinguish friend from foe.

The controls comprise the fire button in the top left and a three-position game speed or skill level control in the bottom right. The game ends when either your three lives have been used up or you hit the maximum score of 199. This was definitely a handheld rather than a pocket-size game at 24 cm × 10.8 cm × 3.8 cm and it requires four AA batteries.

CGL was a British company that was based in London. Their parent company was called Dennis Baylin Trading Ltd and their main business was importing games from manufacturers such as Nintendo and re-badging them as CGL. There are at least seventy-five known games sold under the CGL brand name in the early 1980s. Later, they were briefly owned by Alan Sugar's Amstrad before being shut down.

This type of dedicated electronic game with a VFD screen was long in the tooth by 1982, and more sophisticated LCD games had already pretty much replaced them.

Nintendo Game & Watch (1980)

When Nintendo released their first electronic game in 1980, it was a technological leap forward from the bulky handheld games that had gone before. The confusingly named 'Game & Watch' was so called because included with the single game was a digital clock. Its small size and slim profile was achieved by using a new type of LCD called a segmented display.

It was the brainchild of Gunpei Yokoi, the head of Nintendo Research & Development 1, to produce a pocket calculator-sized device to use on a bus or a train. His idea was to create a toy for adults to pass the time. Yoki and his assistant, Satoru Okada, built a prototype game they called *Ball* and gave it to the electronics company Sharp with the idea to scale it down to calculator size and create the new display.

A juggling game from Nintendo's Game & Watch series. (Courtesy of masatsu, CC BY-SA 2.0)

LCD displays had matured to the point of being able to create segments of any simple shape and these could be switched on and off in sequence to give the illusion of movement. Even so, in 1980, creating a relatively large, animated LCD display was pushing the boundaries of technology to say the least. The device is powered by a 4-bit microprocessor linked to 1,792 bytes of ROM and a tiny 65 bytes of RAM. The screen size is 6.4 cm diagonal and the overall size of the game is only 11.4 cm by 6.4 cm, a size achieved by using small button-sized batteries instead of the AA size required by LED games.

The *Ball* game requires the player to juggle balls, and points are awarded for each catch. The controls move your character left and right to catch, and a ball falling to the ground will break. There are two variations of the game: Game A juggles two balls and Game B, three.

Ball was the first Game & Watch game and was part of the Silver series of single-player, single-screen games in 1980. Over the period 1980 to 1991 another ten series were released, each with different features or improvements. In 1981, static, coloured backgrounds were added as well as an alarm and a gold finish to the case. Also, in 1982, a wide-screen version was produced which had 30 per cent more screen area. From 1983, a series of double-screen versions were introduced, first vertically and later in a horizontal arrangement. The innovative clamshell design both halves the size of the game when folded to fit in your pocket as well as protecting the screens, and the dual screens allow gameplay to cross over from the lower screen to the upper one.

These versions also introduced the cross-shaped controller for screen movement, known as a 'D-pad' – a sort of compact joystick. It was a very easy and efficient way

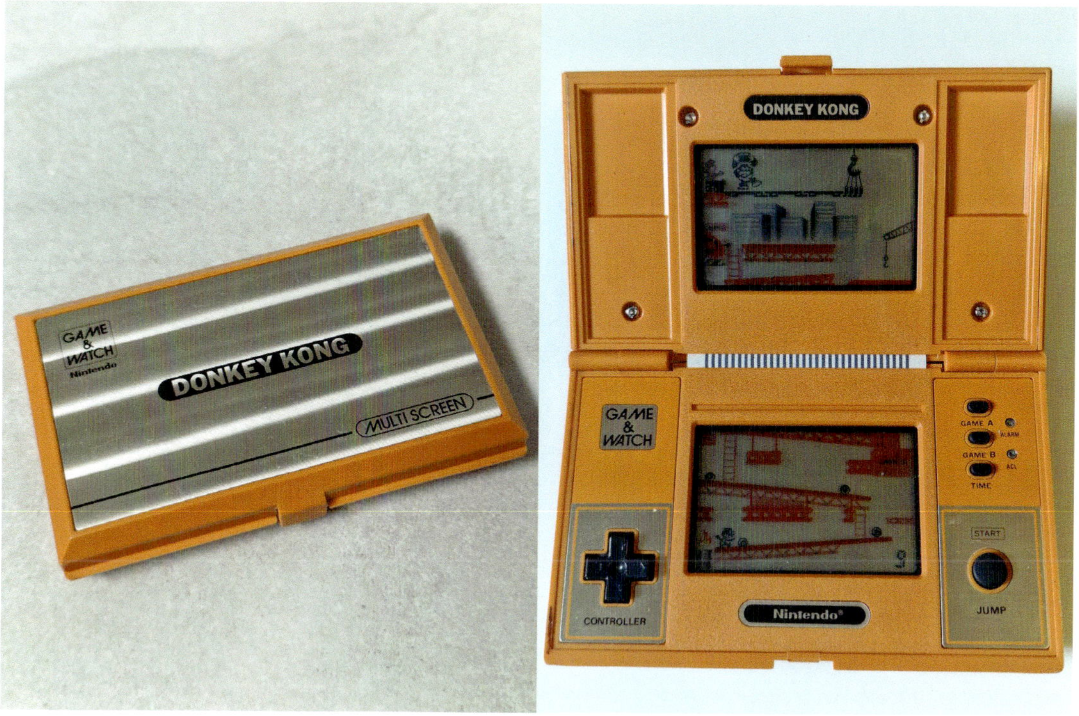

Donkey Kong Game & Watch on a later dual-screen version.

to move around the screen using just pressure from your thumb. The D-pad won a technology award in 2008 and would be used on all of Nintendo's future handheld games.

In all, there were sixty games produced, including *The Legend of Zelda, Super Mario Bros.* and the immensely popular *Donkey Kong*, which sold 8 million units. *Donkey Kong* was created as an arcade game in 1981 by game designer Shigeru Miyamoto for Nintendo. The object of the game is to climb ladders and reach the top of the New York construction site and rescue a lady called Pauline. She is being held captive by the giant gorilla named Donkey Kong who throws barrels at you that have to be avoided by jumping. The climbing and jumping required in the game were new and required real skill to complete the four levels. Its success led to the sequels *Donkey Kong Jr.* and *Donkey Kong 3*.

In the Game & Watch version both screens are used in a game; when Mario reaches the top of the lower screen, he appears in the upper one. All the background scenery of the game – ladders, walkways and buildings – are painted on the glass, with Mario, the barrels and Kong animated using segmented LCDs. In Game A, a point is scored for each barrel jumped; in Game B, the barrels come at you at a faster rate.

The Game & Watch range was a huge success for Nintendo and turned around the company's poor financial situation within a couple of years of launch. Over the next decade, Nintendo went on to sell over 43 million Game & Watches. It was the first of a long line of best-selling games consoles from the company that continue to the present day.

Two Game & Watch titles: *Fire* and *Mario's Cement Factory*.

Tandy *Hold Up* (1983)

We may think that today's video games are a little too violent or non-PC for our younger generation to be playing, but that isn't a new thing. Back in 1983 when Tandy released this bank-robbing game, it caused quite a stir. Playing as the bank robber, you had to keep the three tellers from raising the alarm by using your gun, which was seen as encouraging youngsters into a life of crime. This was a short-lived game and parents who complained were apparently offered a refund of the $19.95 if they returned it.

The Tandy Corporation was formed in the US in 1961 and opened stores on UK high streets from 1973 selling toys, CB radios and other electronic goods under their brand 'Realistic'. In the US, stores were named Radio Shack after Tandy purchased the amateur radio business in 1962.

Tandy got in very early on the home computer boom when they released the TRS-80 in 1977 followed by the Color Computer in 1980. Tandy's personal computer market share was 60 per cent at one point but this declined for various reasons, including an association with the 'cheap' Realistic brand and refusing to allow third parties to develop software for their computers.

But from 1981 to 1992 Tandy made a whole range of electronic games; in fact, around 105 different titles in all. They were a mix of sizes and displays, some LED, some LCD and some tabletop-sized, such as *Alien Chase* where players faced each other with the game between them. *Hold Up* is one of the smaller pocket-sized games, at just 9 cm × 5 cm × 1 cm, and requires two LR44 batteries. Most (if not all) of the games sold by Tandy were made by other manufacturers, such as Bandai, and re-badged as Tandy.

Tandy's fate in the UK was sealed when Carphone Warehouse bought all the UK stores in 1999, closing them down by 2001. However, a new company bought the rights to the brand from Radio Shack in 2012 and Tandy was reborn as an online electronics store, tandyonline.com.

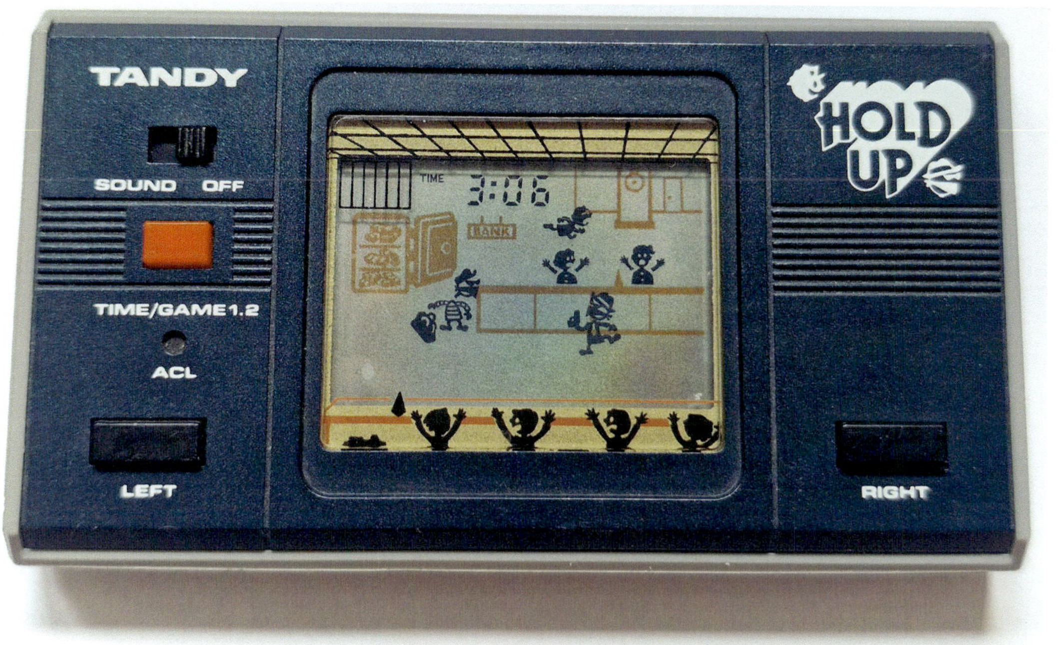

Above: Pocket-sized Tandy *Hold Up*.

Right: Tandy *Shark Island*, 1984, a game where you avoid the sharks and falling coconuts.

2

THE GAME BOY ERA

Throughout most of the 1980s, the screens of pocket-sized games were simple in design. With predefined shapes behind the glass, these could be either lit or not to create simple animations, but this limited each handheld to a single game title. They were not remotely like the full-colour screens of the video arcades. There, characters and icons of any shape and colour could be produced by the software behind them to create realistic animation and the full gaming effect.

But by 1989 technology had advanced to the point where it was possible to fit small dot-matrix screens into games, which, although mostly monochrome, had greatly improved

The Game Boy Pocket, one of the many Game Boy models.

graphics and realism. The screen was now a display area and not specific to the game, which meant that your portable games console could play multiple games on the same device via the use of plug-in cartridges. When you got bored with, say, a tennis game, you could just swap out the cartridge for something with laser cannons. These were known as fourth-generation games and were produced from the early to mid-1990s.

The other distinction from the second generation of the 1970s and 1980s is that they mainly used 16-bit processors, which predominantly made them faster. If you are wondering what happened to the third generation, well, that technology, which used 8-bit processors, was largely used in games consoles that connected to TVs (such as the NES) and not really developed for portables.

Although these fourth-generation games seem primitive by today's standards, they caught the public's imagination and a whole new entertainment genre was born where anyone could while away a train journey or a work break trying to beat your high score. Early favourites were *Tetris*, *Breakout* and *Super Mario Land*, but soon dozens, then hundreds, of titles would become available. The 1990s was the decade when the handheld electronic game became a must-have consumer product. And that product was called the Game Boy.

Nintendo Game Boy (1989)

When the Game Boy was released in Japan in 1989 it was destined to be a success, even a classic. In a time when society was embracing new technology, here was a gadget that was fun, absorbing and filled those boring times on the train or that car journey to school. It was also a way to connect with fellow gaming fans. Its success would lie in the number of different games that would be available, and also in no small part to its long battery life.

Its design started in 1987 when Nintendo's top designer Gunpei Yokoi wanted a successor to the Game & Watch. It would be built around a dot-matrix display, from which its model number of DMG-01 (dot-matrix game) was derived. In 1987, however, LCD dot-matrix display technology was in its infancy, and those available were both expensive and suffered from problems such as ghosting and poor viewing angles. Nintendo almost finalised a deal with Citizen for a monochrome display for ¥1,000 but it fell through at the last minute. Screens from electronics company Sharp were deemed too low quality at the time and so the whole project was very nearly scrapped. However, Yoki soldiered on and learned of a new product in development at Sharp: the super-twisted nematic (STN). Though more expensive, and also having a green tint, it was a far superior product, and a prototype shown to the director gained approval for the go-ahead.

The rest of the hardware also had to be state of the art to give customers the gaming experience that Nintendo desired. At the heart of the Game Boy is a custom chip, the DMG-CPU, which contains all the key graphics and processing components. This comprises an 8-bit processor – the SM83 from Sharp, a GPU (graphics processing unit) – 256 bytes of bootstrap ROM, 127 bytes of RAM and a comprehensive sound generator with four channels. Elsewhere on the compact motherboard is an 8K bank of video RAM for use by the GPU. At the same time as the Game Boy, Nintendo was also working on a home video games console – the Super Nintendo Entertainment System (SNES) – and it was agreed that the Game Boy would use a similar cartridge system.

Left: The original Game Boy.

Below: Inside a Game Boy cartridge, showing the ROM chip and the smaller memory bank controller.

The DMG-CPU interfaces to the game cartridge, known as a Game Boy Game Pak, which contains the video game data. Early cartridges were limited to 32 kilobytes of data due to the 8-bit interface, but this was increased on later cartridges by incorporating memory bank switching within the cartridge, allowing up to 4-megabyte games. There is also a quantity of RAM which was used for saving game progress.

An advert for *The Hunt for Red October*.

The cartridge fits into a slot on the rear of the Game Boy, below which is the battery compartment, which takes four AA batteries. The overall dimensions of 9 cm × 15 cm × 3 cm mean it sits comfortably in the hand and just about fits into a large pocket, and the weight with batteries is around 330 grams.

Rather than just being a rectangular block, the light grey case is designed with a rounded corner on the bottom right below the speaker grille, and a dark grey screen surround with the same corner rounded. On the front are the well-positioned gameplay controls, with the black D-pad on the left side for directional control with a thumb. The A and B buttons in magenta are used for game-dependent actions, such as jumping, and the 'Start' and 'Select' buttons are in light grey. On the right side is a volume thumb wheel and on the left side a screen contrast wheel. There are also three sockets: headphones, charger port and a Game Link for connection to other Game Boys. The Game Link function evolved with successive Game Boy models but was essentially an early networking device. The first multiplayer game released in Japan was *Yakuman*, a version of mah-jong, which allowed players to play each other when connected by a Game Link cable.

Nintendo's aim was for the Game Boy to go on sale for under ¥10,000, but even though the final version had a reduced screen size to save money, it exceeded the target by 25 per cent. However, when it went on sale in Japan on 17 January 1989, the initial production run of 300,000 units sold out within two weeks. Six months later it went on sale in the US for $89 and sold a million in a few weeks. The UK had to wait until the following year and had a purchase price of £99.

It came with the game *Tetris*, which was seen as a game with universal appeal, except in Japan where *Super Mario Land* was one of four games to be bundled with the unit. *Super Mario Land* is a side-scrolling game where your character, Mario, can move left or right using the thumb control, but once the screen scrolls to the right he can't go back. Whilst running, he must jump (using the A button) over enemies to avoid losing a life or jump on top of them for points. There are more points to be collected by reaching those

Super Mario Land game screen.

hanging overhead. The game ends when you have either lost three lives or the timer has reached zero.

Over its lifetime, more than 1,000 games were produced for the original Game Boy. Amongst the most popular were *Tetris*, selling 35 million copies, and the Pokémon series, selling over 46 million. The first Pokémon games were *Pokémon Red Version* and *Pokémon Green Version*, developed in Japan in 1996 and released elsewhere in 1998 and 1999 (with *Green* renamed *Blue*). One of the aims of the game is to collect all 151 Pokémon, with each version having slightly different Pokémon available. Players could then trade them in multiplayer games via Game Link so they could collect them all. *Pokémon* is considered one of the greatest video games of all time and spawned a multi-billion-dollar franchise.

The Game Boy was a great financial success for Nintendo, and they released another three versions with the monochrome screen before they finally got around to a colour version in 1998. By that time, sales had topped 59 million units. One of the reasons for this was the Game Boy's long battery life compared with its competitors. Not that the Game Boy was without its flaws, however. Critics highlighted that there was no backlight for playing in low-light conditions and the display suffered from motion blurring. It was also monochrome when competitors were selling colour consoles. Despite these drawbacks, the Game Boy was, in its day, the best-selling handheld games console by far.

Two popular games.

Top: *Boxxle* – push the boxes onto the dots. Bottom: *Side vs Pocket,* a version of pool.

Bit Corporation Gamate (1990)

The beginning of the 1990s marked a flurry of activity in the handheld market thanks to the success of the Game Boy, with offerings from half a dozen companies wanting a piece of the action. The competition thought that it would be relatively straightforward to improve on Nintendo's offering but were divided on how to do so with the technology available to them at the time. Some went down the route of colour screens, but others, like Taiwanese company Bit Corporation, stuck with monochrome when they brought out a Game Boy rival called the Gamate. In fact, for the Taiwan home market it was called the Super Boy – in case there was any doubt of the company's intentions. With its landscape format, the Gamate doesn't look very much like the Game Boy on the outside, but its screen, internal hardware and controls were all very similar.

When it was released in 1990, Bit Corporation were already a well-established video game company. They had produced games for home consoles like the Atari 2600 and the Nintendo Entertainment System (NES), as well as producing clone systems such as the Bit-90, a version of the ColecoVision. The Gamate was released in most countries around the world, including in the UK where it was distributed by joystick-manufacturer Cheetah at a reasonable £60 and £15 each for the games. It was also later re-released by Maplin with heavily discounted game prices from 99p.

The Gamate from 1990, designed as a competitor for the Game Boy.

So, was it any good? Well, probably the most important component – the screen – sadly wasn't. Though similar in size to the Game Boy's and with the same greenish tint, it suffered from bad motion blur, rendering some games with fast-moving objects impossible to play. Bit Corporation had two different screen suppliers, one slightly less bad than the other. The speaker was also of poor quality. The build quality, however, was very good, with a weighty, solid feel to the case. The internal hardware comprised an 8-bit processor with 16 KB of RAM and 2 KB of ROM and an interface to the credit-card-sized ROM game. On the outside there were ports for earphones, power and a two-way link, and dials for volume and contrast.

On paper the Gamate should have been a rival contender to the Game Boy, but it was the Gamate's games that let it down. Although a respectable seventy titles were released between 1990 and 1995, most were produced by Bit Corporation, with no third-party publishers. The general view is that Bit Corporation's developers were pressured into rushing out the games and the quality suffered as a result. Many games were rip-offs of existing hits, such as *Cube-Up* (*Tetris*), *Bomb Blaster* (*Bomberman*) and *Galaxy Invaders* (*Galaxians*), but were not executed well. This resulted in poor sales, and the resulting financial strain on the company caused them to cease trading in 1992. However, semiconductor manufacturer UMC came to the rescue and took over Gamate production for a while until it ceased for good at the end of 1993.

No accurate sales figures for the Gamate exist, but scarcity of second-hand examples suggest they were quite low. A working example could set you back at least a couple of hundred pounds. So, for collectors of rare and interesting retro tech, owning one of these is a must.

Kung-Fu Fighter game cartridge for the Gamate.

Watara Supervision (1992)

As the popularity of handheld games soared, more manufacturers took note and tried their hand at producing their own versions. This console from Watara, released in 1992, was a copy of the Game Boy for those on a budget. It was hoped that the Supervision, priced at \$49.95 at launch, would steal sales from its Game Boy rival, which cost \$89.99. Its game cartridges were also cheaper.

The Supervision has a similar monochrome screen to the Game Boy at just under 6.4 cm square, and the same set of controls – A, B, Start and Select buttons – plus a four-way movement control. Inside is a low-power version of the popular 6502 microprocessor – the 65C02, running at 4 MHz. It was produced in two different versions: one with a fixed screen and the other with a flexible screen connection, allowing it to be tilted. A unique feature is the ability to output to a TV screen, though this requires an extra adapter. There is also a communications port to create a two-player link, a built-in speaker, a headphone jack with earphones included, a cartridge port and a 6V power adapter.

This all looks pretty good on paper. Even better, when it was released for Christmas 1992 it was \$40 less than a Game Boy. But, as with the Gamate, there were some serious downsides. Firstly, the screen quality wasn't great, with motion blurring due to a lack of hardware acceleration. Secondly, the range and quality of the games were seriously lacking.

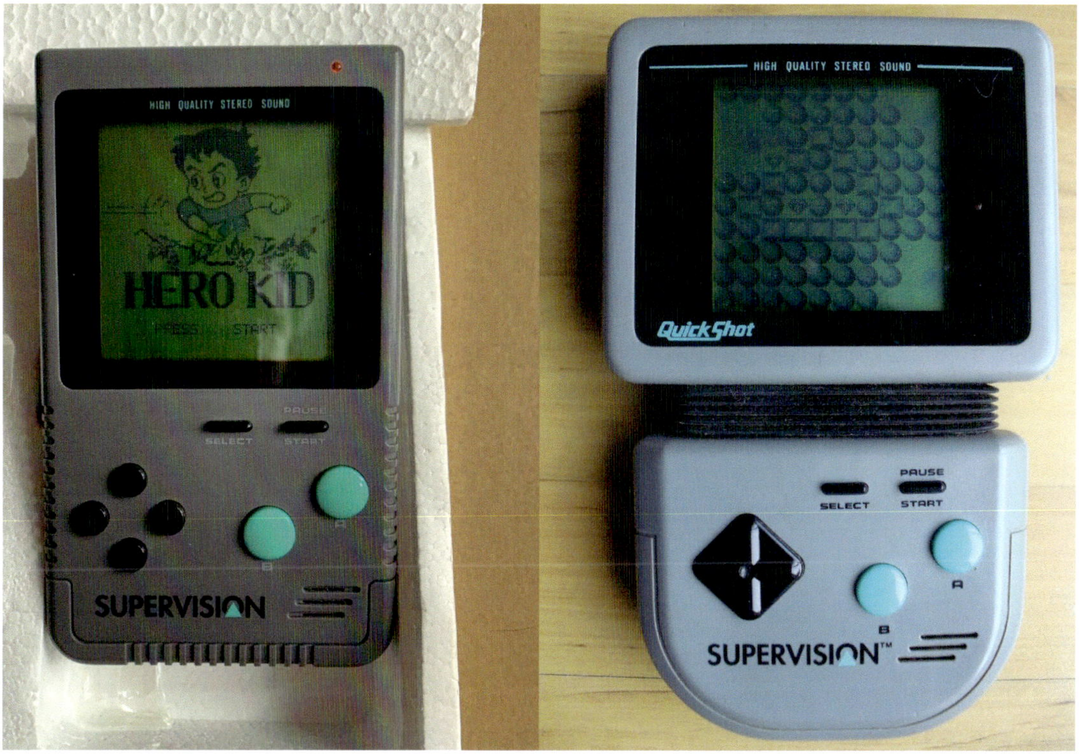

The two versions of the Supervision.

Even though the Supervision was bundled with a version of *Breakout* called *Crystball*, as time went on not nearly enough mainstream games were released for the console. The issue was that Watara didn't engage third-party developers to produce the number and range of games required in order to compete with the Game Boy. Critics said that the games that were produced were 'simplistic'. So, although this budget handheld did attract attention at launch because of its low price, within twelve months or so sales were so low that Watara pulled the plug.

Welback Holdings Mega Duck (1993)

The success of the Game Boy continued to inspire the competition with their own versions, such as this offering from Hong Kong company Welback Holdings. The origin of the name 'Mega Duck' is a mystery, but when it was distributed in South America the company Cougar USA named it the slightly more logical Cougar Boy instead. Although it was also sold in a few European countries, such as France, Germany and Netherlands, it was never marketed in the UK.

In appearance, it bears a strong resemblance to a Game Boy, but with a more rounded case and different-coloured controls. It also has the same ports for charging, headphones and connection to other devices. The similarities continue on the inside where it uses the same SM83 8-bit processor and same 160 × 144-pixel-resolution LCD screen as used by the

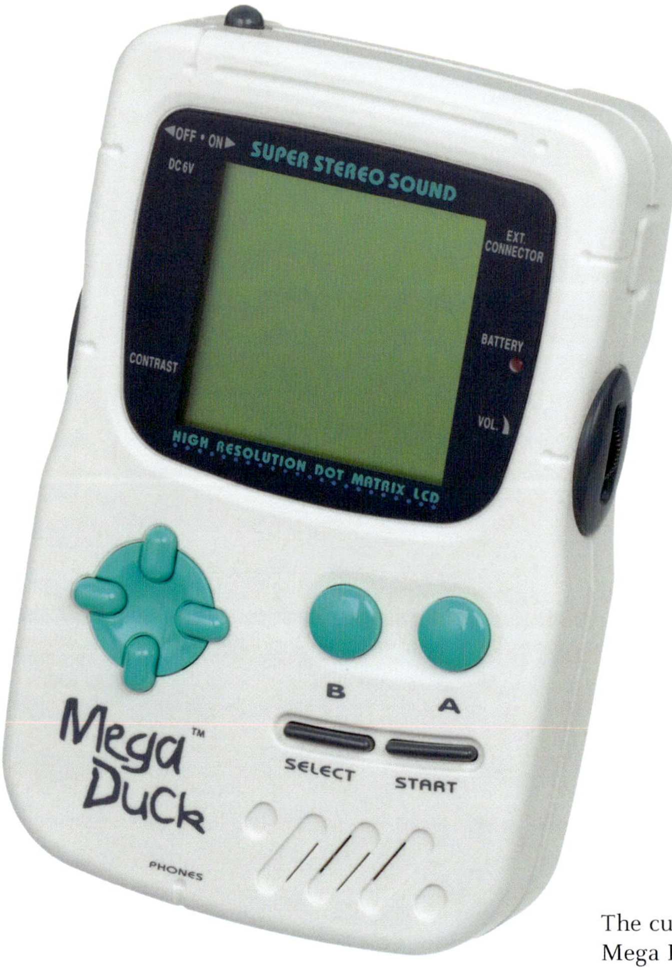

The curiously named Mega Duck.

Game Boy. This enabled games to be ported fairly easily between the two consoles. Game cartridges fit into a thirty-six-pin slot in the rear, and the Mega Duck shipped with a version of *Breakout* called *The Brick Wall.*

There were around twenty-five games released in total and all were developed by the Taiwanese video games company Thin Chen Enterprise under the Sachen brand name. These included titles such as: *Pile Wonder* (like *Boxxle* where you push blocks around the screen), *Snake Roy* (a wizard turns a king into a snake and the king understandably seeks revenge), *Puppet Knight* (a version of *Bomberman*), *Beast Fighter* (your beast character can jump and kick the bad guys) and *Ant Soldiers* (a version of *Lemmings*). The same company also developed for the Nintendo NES, Mega Drive and Game Boy.

Despite these great-sounding games, the Mega Duck was a commercial failure and manufacture ceased in 1993. Reasons cited were the relatively small number of titles available, plus the Game Boy was already well established by this time and had a rather large marketing budget. The Mega Duck is therefore another of the rarer handhelds in the second-hand market today.

Playing *Puppet Knight* on the Mega Duck.

Nintendo Play It Loud! (1995)

By the mid-1990s, even though other competitors had entered the handheld game market, the Game Boy was still the best selling by far. There was also a steady flow of new games titles being released, which kept players loyal. Don't assume that all the players were male either, as a survey in 1995 reported that 46 per cent of Game Boy players were female.

It is perhaps a testament to the Game Boy's success that Nintendo didn't feel the need to update it until nearly six years after the original release. The 'new' version was released on 30 March 1995 and called 'Play It Loud!', though, strangely for a new product, the name didn't appear on the device. You might be forgiven for assuming that the Play It Loud! version would have an updated sound system with a volume wheel that went up to 11. But no, it didn't even have stereo.

The 'Loud' in the name in fact referred to the bright case colours that were available. Instead of the light grey of the original, you could now purchase a Game Boy in red, green, blue, yellow, black, white or clear. With the exception of the black version, the bezel colour was also changed to a dark grey. That was it for the changes. It was perhaps surprising that it took Nintendo such a long time to make a change that was both cheap but appealing to gamers who like to customise their hardware.

Perhaps the reason that Nintendo was slow to release the Play It Loud! was because they were busy developing their home consoles. Nintendo entered the TV games console market back in 1977 when they released the Color TV-Game system. There were five versions in its lifetime, including the Color TV-Game Racing 112 in 1978 which had a steering wheel and gear shift. Although only released in Japan, Nintendo had sold over 3 million units by 1983.

Even more successful was the Famicom ('family computer'), an 8-bit home video games console released in Japan in 1983, whilst in the US and Europe it was renamed the Nintendo Entertainment System (NES). With its major games titles such as *Super Mario Bros.* and *The Legend of Zelda*, it became the number-one-selling console in Japan and the US.

Above: 'Play It Loud!' editions came in various bright colours.

Left: Nintendo advert for their *Toy Story* game, 1996.

Nintendo Game Boy Pocket (1996)

The Pocket edition of the Game Boy saw the first real changes since the release of the original, seven years earlier. The case size was reduced by 25 mm in height and 12 mm in width. It was also 7 mm slimmer – hence the 'Pocket' name.

Inside, there were some minor but worthwhile improvements. A new screen was fitted which, although of the same size, had reduced ghosting and removed the greenish tinge of the original.

On the minus side, its smaller size meant that there was only space for two of the smaller AAA batteries, which reduced battery life from thirty to ten hours. Other changes were a smaller Game Link port, a new SoC (system on a chip) with internal video memory and removal of the battery power LED (although this was reinstated the following year). Of course, in terms of game cartridges, the Pocket version was fully compatible with the original Game Boy, and its release in Japan in July 1996 was timed to coincide with the launch of *Pokémon* which boosted sales. Initially it was launched with a silver case, but six months later other case colours – red, green, blue, gold, yellow, clear and black – were available.

The Game Boy Pocket was broadly welcomed with its less ghosty, more playable screen, but also faced criticism for still being monochrome when other competitors were offering colour. Also, one of Game Boy's big attractions – its long battery life – had been reduced by two-thirds to just ten hours.

A clear-case version of the Game Boy Pocket.

An advert from 1996 offering the Pocket version for £49.99.

Tiger Electronics Game.com (1997)

The Game.com, released in 1997, was designed by US toy maker Tiger Electronics, who are perhaps best known today for the Furby – the robotic owl-like creature that was the must-have toy for Christmas 1998. The Game.com was a departure from the conventional handheld games console in that it was marketed towards professionals. As well as a games machine, the Game.com was also a simple personal digital assistant (PDA) with a calendar, phone directory and calculator.

In the 1990s, digital organisers were all the rage and the market was dominated by the likes of Psion with their 3c and 3mx models of the late 90s. The PDA started off as a replacement for the paper Filofax, but added more and more features such as agendas, spreadsheets and databases. The Game.com had basic internet connectivity (hence the '.com' in the name) via a 14.4 Kbit modem which allowed text-based web pages and emails, though they could not be saved. The modem was plugged into one of the two slots on the rear, the other slot being available for games cartridges. Tiger hoped that it would go

The first handheld console with a touchscreen.

head-to-head with the Game Boy. Although the Game.com screen was monochrome and not backlit, its secret weapon was that it was a touchscreen and games could be played using a stylus instead of conventional button controls. It was also cheaper than the Game Boy, being priced at £79.99 when launched in the UK at the end of 1997.

The built-in game was *Solitaire* and eventually the games library grew to around twenty, many of which were more cerebral games like *Wheel of Fortune*, *Scrabble* and *Jeopardy*. These worked well with the touchscreen, but action-based games suffered from bad screen blur. Although games could not use the internet, there was a port to connect two consoles together in a multiplayer mode. In 1999, a budget version was released: the Pocket Pro. It lacked internet capability and had a smaller case and screen, only one cartridge slot and sold for just $30.

The Game.com was definitely a jack-of-all-trades machine, though unfortunately it didn't do any of them well. Even though it had great sound and was the first handheld to have a touchscreen and internet, it did not fare well against the Game Boy and both models were discontinued in 2000.

Nintendo Game Boy Light (1998)

Two years after the Pocket edition, Nintendo launched another updated version of the Game Boy, although it was only released in Japan. It was named not because it was lightweight or light on features, but because this model had a backlight for the first time.

It had always been a drawback of previous Game Boys that they could not be played in the dark (under the bed covers for instance); even low-light conditions could be a problem. There was a contrast wheel on the side but that didn't really help at all. A partial solution had been to invest in a magnifier/backlight accessory, which comprised a square

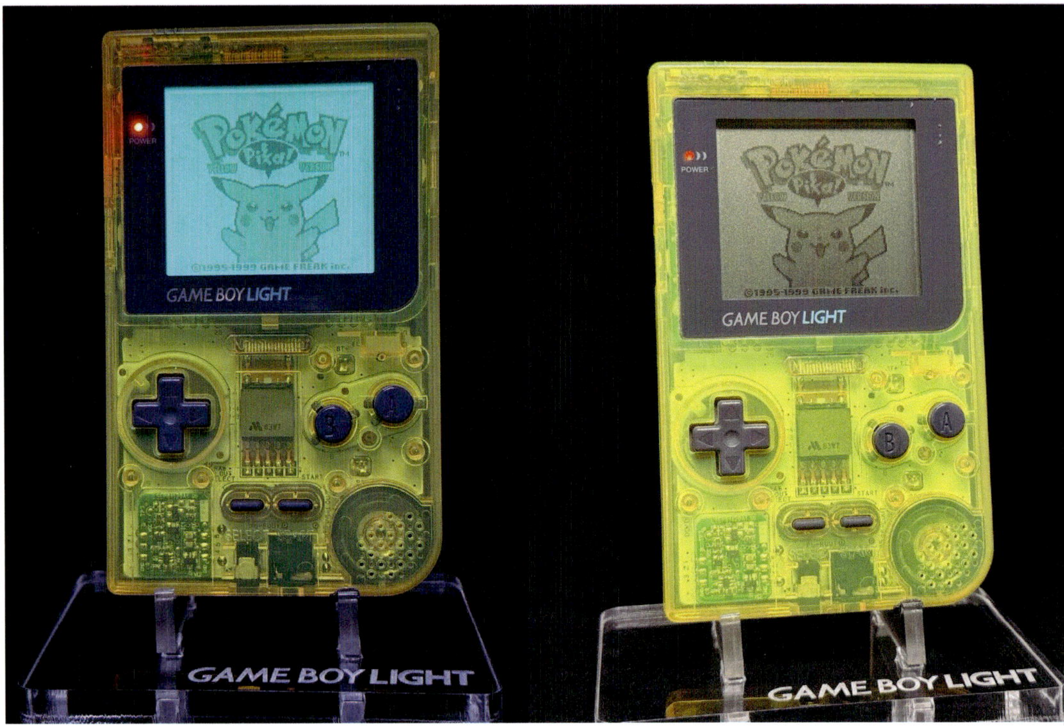

The first Game Boy model with a backlit screen.

magnifying glass with lamps at either side to fit over the screen and provide illumination in the dark. This was not ideal as the lamps were in front of the screen and caused reflections and uneven lighting. The Game Boy Light with its backlit screen solved the problem once and for all. It was actually a bluish-green glow because it used an electroluminescent backlight – the same as used in some digital watches of the time.

However, the light meant more power from the batteries and so the Light required an extra AA battery. As these were larger than those in the Pocket edition, the case was increased in size slightly to accommodate them. The light was selected by an extra position on the on-off switch on the top and, when in use, the batteries lasted around twelve hours instead of twenty.

This was the last tweak to the original Game Boy, as an all-new colour version was released the same year. But prior to that, the various monochrome Game Boys had sold over 59 million units worldwide as of 30 September 1997.

3

GAMING GETS COLOURFUL

The advent of colour screens for electronic games was revolutionary. They now took on an extra dimension, using colour to draw realistic characters, paint more interesting backgrounds and differentiate the good guys from the bad. Colour was a literal gamechanger.

However, like most new technologies, colour LCD screens didn't take over immediately but evolved over time. They were first developed in Japan by Seiko for portable LCD televisions. Seiko even produced a colour TV watch as early as 1982, although it did need to be connected to a separate receiver. But the picture quality was poor and it took another decade of development before LCD colour TVs became a practical alternative to CRT screens.

In the world of handheld electronic games, colour screens also took over gradually rather than at a particular point in time. Even though the first electronic game with a colour screen was available in 1989, Nintendo stuck with their monochrome-screened Game Boy for

Nintendo's Game Boy finally gets a colour screen.

A Nintendo 3DS with two colour screens.

nearly ten years. This was because initially colour screens were much more expensive, and, perhaps more importantly, they consumed a lot of power and so were hard on battery life.

Despite these drawbacks, a number of competitors stepped up to take on the Game Boy. In the early to mid-1990s the monochrome Game Boy came under increasing attack from rivals who wanted to topple its dominance in the handheld gaming market. The main contenders were Atari, who released their pioneering Lynx machine in 1989, and Nintendo's rival Sega, who released their advanced Game Gear a year later. These were heavyweights with new, superior technology and on paper at least made the Game Boy look a little old fashioned. It was not until 1998 that Nintendo finally brought their own colour machine to the market.

Atari Lynx (1989)

The Atari Lynx was the first handheld game console with a colour LCD screen, and so after a prototype was shown at the Consumer Electronics Show in January 1989, its official launch was eagerly awaited.

Atari Inc. was a US company founded in California in 1972 by Nolan Bushnell and Ted Dabney. They were one of the pioneers of both arcade video games and home computers

The Lynx, Atari's first handheld console.

in the 1970s and 1980s. Their first success was the arcade game *Pong*, followed by a version for the home TV. Atari then released a series of TV games consoles, starting with the Atari 2600 in 1977. In 1985, they entered the personal computer market with their Atari ST range of advanced colour 16/32-bit machines. With their track record, you would have expected Atari to produce something special when they entered the handheld market in 1989.

The Lynx was designed by two former Amiga engineers, R. J. Mical and Dave Needle, at US software company Epyx, but when Epyx didn't have the cash to complete the project Atari stepped in to do the manufacturing and marketing. The result was an advanced machine for the time with several innovative features. The colour screen is a landscape format of 7 cm × 4.4 cm and a resolution of 160 × 102. Cleverly, if you are left-handed, the screen can be flipped 180 degrees so you can use the 'cross' button with your other thumb. It also has the useful backlight and it can be turned off to save the batteries. The controls were pretty standard for the time, with buttons to power on and off, for the backlight and for the screen flip (which also doubles as a pause button). The A and B buttons are duplicated for when the console is being played the other way up.

Even though the Lynx was classed as a fourth-generation machine in that it still has an 8-bit processor like the Game Boy, it has some nifty hardware to speed up drawing of graphics. This is done in a custom VLSI (very large-scale integration) chip on the motherboard nicknamed 'Suzy'. Suzy performs a lot of the heavy lifting when it comes to drawing graphics on the screen. The hardware could copy figures known as 'sprites' – 2D graphics objects made up from simple triangles or polygons – very quickly from memory to screen, as well as performing stretching, zooming, and collision detection, taking the burden off the CPU and allowing it to do the gameplay. All of this just speeds up the on-screen graphics and makes the games more playable.

Another VLSI chip, nicknamed 'Mikey', running at 16 MHz, contains a version of a MOS 6502 processor, four-channel sound generation, a driver for the LCD display (sixteen colours could be used simultaneously out of a palette of 4,096) and 512 bytes of bootstrap ROM for loading the game cartridge. The game code has to be copied into the 64K RAM on board before it can be run. There is also a ComLynx port to allow up to eight Lynxes to be connected together in a multiplayer mode.

There were around seventy-three games produced for the Lynx over its lifetime. Some were recognisable versions of classics, such as *Ms. Pac Man*; others not so, like *Rampart, Scrapyard Dog, Turbos Sub, A.P.B.* and *Dirty Larry: Renegade Cop*; and some were inspired by film franchises, such as *Batman Returns* and *Bill & Ted's Excellent Adventure.*

When launched in the US on 1 September 1989 at the introductory price of $180, it was well received even though it was twice the price of the Game Boy, which had been released five months earlier. Two years later, Atari released the Lynx II for $99. There were several minor improvements such as a sleeker case, stereo sound and better battery life.

The Lynx had its fans, but ultimately it failed when it came up against the well-established Game Boy and also competition from Sega. When it was finally discontinued in 1995 it had sold around 2 million units. More recently, Atari has been recognised as a pioneer of handheld game development and some Lynx games have been re-released and even ported to other platforms. If you want to get your hands on one for yourself, they can be found on auction sites from around £100.

The motherboard showing 'Mikey' (the big square chip) and the smaller 'Suzy'.

Above: The later Lynx II playing *Hard Drivin'*.

Right: A Lynx game cartridge and the game in play.

Sega Game Gear (1990)

A year after the release of the Lynx, the Japanese video game company Sega produced their own colour-screen console, the Game Gear, in an attempt to win a share of the handheld market. Although it was a similar design to the Lynx, the Game Gear's primary competitor would be Nintendo's Game Boy, which by this time had enjoyed ten years of dominance.

The Sega Corporation dates back to 1960 and had its origins in coin-operated games. But in the early 1980s, Sega started to develop home video game consoles and became a rival to Nintendo. In 1986, Sega released their Master System in Japan, and Europe a year

Sega's first handheld games console: the Game Gear.

later. Although sales in the US and Japan were poor, by 1990 the Master System outsold the Nintendo Entertainment System (NES) in the UK by nearly two to one, and it went on to be the basis of the successful Sega Mega Drive.

The Game Gear was Sega's first foray into the handheld market and had a lot of catching up to do. To speed up development, much of the Game Gear's hardware was derived from the existing Master System. It used the same Z80 8-bit processor and Texas Instruments sound generator, which output through the single speaker or stereo via headphones. The display is an 8.1-cm, backlit, colour LCD with 160 × 144-pixel resolution and the ability to display thirty-two colours simultaneously from a palette of 4,096. Nintendo's dominance of the games market meant they held exclusive rights for many titles and consequently third-party developers were unable to create games for Sega. But fortunately for Sega, basing it on their Master System meant that existing games could be relatively easily translated for use in the portable console.

At the Game Gear launch there were six titles available, including their best-seller *Land of Illusion Starring Mickey Mouse*. Another big hit was *Sonic the Hedgehog* by game developer Ancient. It was released in 1991 for both the Game Gear and Master System, and was highly acclaimed by the industry critics. Over its lifetime, the Game Gear had more than 300 titles released. Out of the box, it came bundled with a version of *Tetris* called *Columns*, where you have to manipulate a falling column of three different symbols in an attempt to align them with the same symbols below. If you already owned a Master System, your Game Gear could play its cartridges directly if you purchased their Master Gear adapter. Other accessories were a TV tuner to turn the console into a television, and an adapter to plug into a car's cigarette lighter.

Two titles for the Game Gear.

Like the Lynx, the Game Gear's horizontal layout is generally accepted as being easier to play than vertical consoles like the Game Boy. It was slightly smaller and lighter than the Lynx, even though it required the same six AA batteries. These suffered from the demands of the colour screen and backlight and had to be replaced every three to five hours, compared with thirty hours for the Game Boy! However, the Game Gear was marketed as being superior to the Game Boy in every way.

Sega's advertising not only attacked Game Boy directly, but also their customers, with one advert likening them to dogs, who are colour blind, or having a low IQ! Nintendo was not impressed, but Sega's tactics didn't help Game Gear sales.

On arrival to the UK in 1991, the Game Gear was competitively priced at £99 and around £20 for a game cartridge. Its success depends on how you measure it. It outsold the Lynx and in terms of absolute sales, it reached a very respectable 10.6 million in 1996. This was the best amongst landscape-format consoles. Also, at its peak in late 1992, Sega had 40 per cent market share of handhelds. But, crucially, the Game Boy had a big head start and once it had a commanding share of the market, it was hard for competitors to take it back from Nintendo.

Despite its many advantages over the Game Boy – a backlight, colour screen, a good games library and a lower price – Sega didn't produce a successor to the Game Gear after it was discontinued in 1997. However, in 2020, as part of Sega's sixtieth anniversary celebrations, the company produced the Game Gear Micro, a retro console with a 2.8-cm screen and powered by batteries or USB.

Above: Magazine adverts for the Game Gear and the *Super Space Invaders* game.

Below: Sega Master System and Sega Master System II.

NEC TurboExpress (1990)

The TurboExpress (known as the PC Engine GT in Japan) from the NEC Corporation was the most advanced handheld on the market when released in December 1990. Though not officially available in Europe, it was the most expensive handheld amongst its rivals in Japan and the US at ¥44,800/$250 (around £450 at today's prices).

The NEC Corporation is a global electronics and communications company founded in 1899 in Tokyo. They were an early developer of personal computers and dominated the Japanese market in the 1980s. They were also a leading semiconductor manufacturer. In 1987, they entered the home video games market with the PC-Engine, known as the TurboGrafx-16 in the US, and it was this machine that became the basis for their TurboExpress handheld games console.

Though it was an upright console like the Game Boy, it was much bigger and heavier, partly due to the fact that it required six AA batteries. But its power consumption was so great that even this power pack would only last around three hours! Purchase of a mains adapter was therefore pretty much essential, though it then lost its portability.

Inside, there is a HuC6280 microprocessor by Japanese company Hudson Soft, as used in the TurboGrafx-16 console. The name implied it was a 16-bit machine, but this just referred to the machine's 16-bit architecture. The microprocessor itself was an improved version of the 8-bit MOS Technology 6502. The backlit LCD screen was cutting edge at the time. Though only 6.6 cm on the diagonal, it had an improved resolution over its rivals of 400 × 270 pixels. The graphics hardware was also impressive and capable of displaying sixty-four sprites simultaneously of up to 481 colours out of a palette of 512.

The TurboExpress from NEC.

On the outside there are the usual direction control and gameplay buttons, but with the addition of two turbo switches, which essentially speed up the response of the controls to assist the player.

There are also ports for power, headphones and for a TurboLink cable to link to another machine for a two-player mode. However, games that supported this, such as *Bomberman '93*, were few and far between. There was also a TurboVision TV tuner adapter for $100 for watching TV on your games console. And in case you wanted to use it as a video monitor, there was also a composite video input.

So, the TurboExpress had some advantages: a hi-res colour screen and a ready-made games library from the TurboGrafx-16 console. However, there were more negatives than positives. Firstly, the price, which actually went up to $300 for a while after launch to cover increased production costs. Then there was the short battery life, which was an ongoing cost after purchase. Finally, any games from the TurboGrafx-16 with text, such as role playing, would not play well on the smaller screen as the text wasn't scaled. It wasn't a financial disaster by any means, selling around 1.5 million units, but it was NEC's only foray into the portable games market. The TurboExpress was discontinued in 1994 and NEC left the video games industry in 1998.

Interesting fact: a TurboExpress appears in the 1998 film *Enemy of the State*. As they were not available in Europe, they are a rare find and to own one today would cost around £500.

A TurboGrafx-16 video console playing *Konami*.

Sega Nomad (1995)

The Sega Nomad (also known as Genesis Nomad) was another instance of a portable being based on an existing home video console, in this case the Sega Genesis. The Genesis was a successful home video console from 1989 that was better known as the Mega Drive outside the US. The Mega Drive in turn was a replacement for Sega's Master System. The Nomad was only available in the US and when launched in October 1995, it would have cost around $179.

Externally the Nomad has the standard thumb movement controller on the left side and a collection of gameplay buttons on the right (marked A, B, C and X, Y, Z) for compatibility with Genesis games. On the top is an 'AV out' for connection to a TV, alongside the rather large cartridge slot and a 'DC in' port for an AC adapter. This was a must because, as with all these early portables, the six AA batteries would only last for a disappointing two or three hours.

The Nomad's hardware is nearly identical to the Genesis video console, with the exception, of its 8.2-cm backlit LCD screen. Internally, it uses the same Motorola 68000 – a hybrid 16/32-bit processor – which has registers that are 32 bits wide but connects to the outside world via a 16-bit bus. Generally, the more bits, the faster the data can be moved around, resulting in speedier games.

The Nomad was slightly unusual in that it didn't have its own games library. Instead, it only played Genesis games, but there were eventually over 500 to choose from. One of Sega's most successful was *Sonic the Hedgehog*, released on the Genesis in 1991.

Was the Nomad a success? In a word – no, despite sales of around 1 million. Although there was praise for it at the launch, citing its impressive games library, there were also several drawbacks. Firstly, the price was relatively high, but equally important was its short battery life – the Achilles heel of these early colour handhelds. Also, Genesis games with text to read, such as role-playing games (RPGs), were not easy to play on the small screen. Sega continued with the Nomad until 1999, when they pulled the plug to concentrate on their home video game consoles.

Sega's Nomad handheld with a Sonic cartridge plugged in the top.

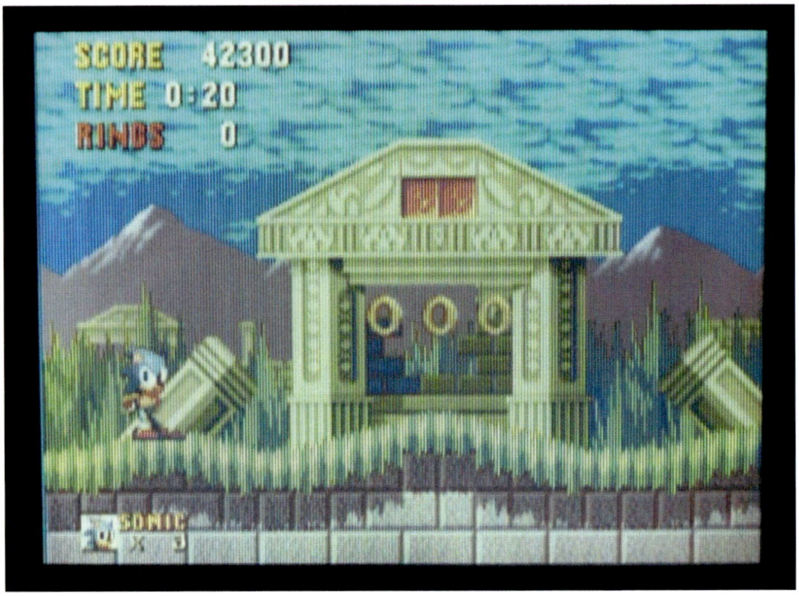

A Nomad playing *Sonic the Hedgehog*.

SNK Neo Geo Pocket Color (1999)

This pocket gaming console from arcade game manufacturer SNK had the same horizontal orientation as Sega's consoles but had a couple of key differences. Firstly, the LCD screen wasn't backlit and so needed fairly good ambient lighting for games to be playable. The upside of this, though, was that without the power required for the light, the batteries lasted a respectable forty hours. Another improvement was the addition of an eight-way mini joystick for direction control with the thumb. This gave more precise control than the D-pad controls fitted to most other consoles at the time.

SNK were founded in Japan in 1986 and initially released a monochrome version of the Neo Geo in 1998, but by the end of the decade most manufacturers had moved over to colour screens and SNK had to follow suit. By the time the colour version was released in Europe in October 1999, SNK had already produced a third, slightly slimmed-down version for the Japanese market called the New Neo Geo Pocket Color. Its 6.6-cm screen can display 146 colours simultaneously with a resolution of 160 × 152 pixels. Inside, it is powered by a TLCS-900 Toshiba processor, which is based on the Z80 from Zilog and runs at 6 MHz. There are also some PDA-style features such as a clock and a calendar and there is a CR2032 coin battery for saved game data and to power the clock when switched off.

The games library for the Neo Geo was actually pretty good, with seventy-three titles produced during the console's short lifetime. Though most were by SNK, there were a few others from third-party developers, such as a version of *Pac-Man* from Namco and the highly rated *Sonic the Hedgehog Pocket Adventure* from Sega.

The Neo Geo Pocket Color actually had a lot going for it, and was a competent machine with no major drawbacks. It stood up well against the competition at the time, mainly the WonderSwan from Bandai and Nintendo's Game Boy Color, and sold 100,000 units in its first year. However, in 2001, possibly before it could reach its full potential, SNK got into

The Neo Geo Pocket Color in blue and the slimmer New Neo Geo Pocket Color above.

financial difficulties and went bankrupt. Although SNK's franchises and games licences lived on and were sold to other companies, the Neo Geo was discontinued and it was the end of the line for the Neo Geo Pocket Color.

Nintendo Game Boy Color (1998)

It was a long time coming, but in November 1998 gamers in Europe could finally purchase a colour version of the beloved Game Boy. A colour-screen variant was first conceived back in the early 1990s when Nintendo's Research & Development 1 (R&D1) department, headed by Satoru Okada, produced a prototype based on a 32-bit processor. However, interest in colour was shelved until 1997 when a rival – Bandai – leaked news of a new colour console. This was big news because the designer was none other than Gunpei Yokoi, the former Nintendo employee who had developed the original Game Boy alongside Satoru Okada. Bandai's WonderSwan panicked Nintendo into reviving Okada's original prototype and getting something to market ASAP. The Game Boy Color was the result, but sadly it lacked the powerful 32-bit processor due to a lack of development time.

Playing *Tetris DX*.

Essentially, they just added a colour screen to the original Game Boy, which, given how old the original model was, would seem like a missed opportunity. However, there was an upside. Owners of previous monochrome models would still be able to play all the games they had already purchased on the new colour model.

Physically, it measures 13.3 cm × 8 cm × 2.9 cm and weighs just 542 grams. This makes it almost identical in size to the Game Boy Light, though the screen is slightly smaller at 5.7 cm diagonal. The screen resolution is the same as previous Game Boy models to allow for game compatibility, but there is no backlight, which helps to prolong battery life.

Inside, there is an updated system on a chip (SoC), called the CPU GBC, containing the CPU, GPU (graphics processing unit) with 16K of video RAM and a bootstrap ROM for the code that is run on startup. The CPU – a Sharp SM83 – is the same 8-bit processor and same speed as the original Game Boy. This allows old games to run but new games could run in a 'double-speed' mode of 8.4 MHz. New games could also utilise 32 KB of RAM – four times the amount of the old Game Boy.

The case has the same controls on the front, a D-pad and four control buttons, with a volume wheel and a Game Link port (of a smaller design than previous) on the side. There is an infrared port on the top for wireless data transfer and the game slot on the rear for cartridges of up to 8 MB of ROM.

Like the Play It Loud! model, the case came in five colours (as per the coloured letters of 'COLOR' on the front), which are Berry, Grape, Kiwi, Dandelion and Teal. There was also a translucent case in Atomic Purple, plus some special editions such as Pokémon Pikachu.

Clear-case Game Boy Colour and a Pikachu special edition.

As well as being able to play existing monochrome games, many of these were reworked for the Game Boy Color, adding new levels and features, and were often denoted by the 'DX' (deluxe) suffix. One of these was *Tetris DX*, available at launch and one of the most popular titles. Another was *Super Mario Bros. DX*, which was a big seller for the NES, and with the Game Boy Color's colour graphics and speed, a more faithful version was created. But the most successful new games were in the Pokémon series, such as *Pokémon Crystal, Pokémon Silver* and *Pokémon Gold*, which really helped to boost sales.

The Game Boy Color's screen was undoubtedly very good, with a rich colour palette and smooth motion, and it sold extremely well. However, it wasn't perfect and some commentators said the colours could look a bit dull. There was also the lack of backlight and relatively short battery life.

This was the last of the Game Boy line, which had debuted over a decade earlier. By the time the Game Boy Color was discontinued in 2003, total Game Boy sales had reached a staggering 119 million – more than any other game console at the time. Nintendo were not going to rest on their laurels, though, and it would be only a couple of years before a completely new console was launched.

A scene from the game *The Mummy*.

Advert for *Legend of Zelda: Link's Awakening DX* and *WarioLand II* (1999).

4

INTO THE TWENTY-FIRST CENTURY

Although the technology used in both home video and portable games consoles evolved fairly steadily, the industry likes to split the timeline into categories that are called 'generations'. For example, when the TurboGrafx-16 was released in 1987, this was heralded as the start of the fourth generation of consoles because there was a move to more powerful 16-bit processors from the previous 8-bit machines (see Appendix). The Genesis Nomad, Game Boy Color and Neo Geo, amongst others, belong to the fifth generation, which commenced in the mid-1990s.

By the start of the millennium, game consoles continued to benefit from the downward cost of electronic components and therefore contained more powerful processors and larger amounts of memory. This in turn lead to more complex games, with smoother, higher-definition graphics and greater depth of colours. More complex electronics together

A Nintendo DS Lite from 2006.

with bigger and brighter screens placed greater demands on the batteries, but battery capacity improved when internal lithium-ion rechargeables became standard.

The main handheld players of this period would also be the big names in home video game consoles, i.e. Nintendo and Sony, although other companies made some interesting devices. Many, if not all, of the games developed for home consoles of the time, such as the Sony PlayStation and the Nintendo GameCube, were also released for the portable market. These include the racing game series Need for Speed, the action-adventure Grand Theft Auto franchise, Tony Hawk's skateboarding series and the stealth action-adventure Metal Gear series of games.

The beginning of the twenty-first century marks the start of the sixth generation of video game consoles, for both home and portable consoles. This generation heralded the start of online gaming, and in 1998 Sony released their Dreamcast home console with the first modem. At this time, internet connection was via a hardwired phone line, so this wasn't a practical option with portables. Handheld consoles needed Wi-Fi before they could have their own online experience, so they would have to wait until 2004. The first handheld console of the sixth generation was the Bandai WonderSwan.

Bandai WonderSwan (1999)

In 1994, Japanese video game company Bandai linked up with Apple (yes, the makers of the iPhone) to produce the Apple Pippin gaming console. Its unique selling point (USP) was that it had a modem for the internet, but when it was released in 1996 it was a commercial failure. Undaunted, Bandai tried again, this time with a handheld games console to beat the Game Boy. To create it, they recruited none other than the designer of the original Game Boy, Gunpei Yokoi.

Unusually, the console would be monochrome when others were turning to colour. Bandai thought that, like the best-selling Game Boy, it would still sell well if it was fast,

The Bandai WonderSwan Color.

had a good battery life and a low price. There were also no less than nine funky case colours available, including metallic finishes, and two-tone special editions. The console was named the WonderSwan because in Japan swans are seen as being both elegant and powerful.

Sadly, Yoki died in a car accident in 1997 before completion, but the project continued and the WonderSwan was unveiled in Tokyo a year later in October 1998. It was released for sale in Japan the following March. Bandai took the questionable decision not to launch outside Japan – possibly because of an overcrowded handheld market.

The WonderSwan had some good things going for it. As well as the impressive forty hours of battery life, at its heart was a 16-bit processor – the first to be fitted into a handheld. This gave it a performance advantage over its 8-bit rivals of the time. Another novel feature was the ability to switch the 6.4-cm-diagonal screen between portrait and landscape modes – hence the dual set of controls.

But was it enough to compete with its rivals? Just a few months earlier, Nintendo had released its Game Boy Color and so Bandai was already on the back foot. They therefore started work on a colour version: the WonderSwan Color, which was released in December the following year.

The Color model is slightly larger than the original at 12.8 cm × 7.4 cm × 2.4 cm and has a larger 7.4-cm-diagonal screen but with the same 224 × 144 resolution to retain backwards compatibility with existing games, though battery life is reduced to fifteen hours from the single AA battery.

Games titles for the WonderSwan were produced by several well-known developers, such as Taito (of *Space Invaders* fame), Namco (*Galaxian, Pac-Man*) and SquareSoft (*Final Fantasy*). Final Fantasy is a franchise with sixteen role-playing games (RPGs) in the main series to date. Each instalment has different characters and a different plot but all have some similar elements and themes and feature a group of heroes who have to battle against evil.

The WonderSwan had some success in that the colour version alone sold 1.1 million units. And in 2002, a third model with mainly cosmetic changes – the SwanCrystal – was released. By this time, though, Nintendo had released their new Game Boy Advance and, despite the SwanCrystal being priced at ¥1,000 less, it marked the start of a steep decline in their sales. It also didn't help that by then SquareSoft had withdrawn support for the WonderSwan. The entire WonderSwan range was discontinued in 2003, putting an end to Bandai producing games hardware.

Game Boy Advance (2001)

All previous Game Boy models had been portrait-orientated, so to change the Game Boy Advance (GBA) to a landscape-playable format might have seemed like a big step for Nintendo. However, other manufacturers were making the same move, and it was a natural consequence of screen shapes changing from portrait to the more familiar widescreen in a 3:2 or 16:9 ratio. But also, placing the controls either side of the screen seems a more comfortable layout. As well as the D-pad and A and B buttons, two extra controls – L and R – were placed on the 'shoulders' of the console. While not everyone liked them at the time, they are now a standard feature on handhelds and games controllers.

The original Game Boy Advance playing *Jonny Moseley Mad Trix.*

Rather than being a step change in the gaming experience, the GBA was more of an incremental move in the evolution of Nintendo's portable console line. There were some improvements, but there was a lot that was familiar. New GBA games made use of the bigger screen and better performance, but backwards compatibility meant that owners of any of the previous Game Boys could still play their old games. Not only was the screen bigger than the Game Boy Color at 7.4 cm diagonal, it had an improved resolution of 260 × 140 pixels, though games for previous Game Boy models would not use the full screen size as they were created for a lower resolution. Also, as the GBA didn't have a backlight, it suffered from the familiar problem of being difficult to see the screen unless played in a well-lit environment.

The two AA batteries would give around fifteen hours of play, and this was the last model to use them; future models went to an internal, larger-capacity rechargeable battery. There was a power adapter available, and other accessories included a GBA Link Cable to connect to another GBA or the GameCube console.

As well as a new look, there were some useful changes under the bonnet too. The processor was a powerful 32-bit RISC chip by Arm Holdings: an ARM7 running at over 16 MHz. The ARM7 is from a family of processors used widely in the portables industry (most smartphones have one) and the ARM7TDMI model uses internal 32-bit registers for speed but interfaces to the motherboard though a 16-bit bus. It is contained within a custom system on a chip (SoC) called the CPU AGB. Alongside this processor power, there was a more sophisticated graphics processor to take care of all the sprite drawing, colour processing and general trickery to make the graphics animation slick and colourful.

To enable backwards compatibility with 8-bit game cartridges, the SoC also contained the 8-bit Sharp SM83 processor used in the previous Game Boys. On detection of an old cartridge, this processor runs the game software. The new cartridges were half the height of the previous design.

An upgraded Game Boy Advance with a modern backlit screen.

As well as being backwards compatible with games from all Game Boy generations, games from popular series such as Super Mario and Pokémon were re-released for the GBA, for example *Super Mario Advance* and *Pokémon Emerald,* to take advantage of its increased performance. *Pokémon Ruby* and *Pokémon Sapphire* were best-selling games. At the European launch there were fifteen new titles available, including *Top Gear GT Championship, Fire Pro Wrestling, Mr. Driller 2* and *Super Dodge Ball Advance.*

It went on sale in March 2001 and two months later in North America for the price of $99. It was generally well received, with praise for the GBA's graphics capabilities and larger screen. The only real criticism was the dim screen under normal lighting conditions.

Sales, however, exceeded expectations and once again showed Nintendo's dominance and lack of lasting competition in the handheld games market. In the UK alone, in the first week of launch 81,000 units were sold, beating the previous record held by the PlayStation 2 in 2000.

In a radical redesign in 2003, Nintendo released the Game Boy Advance SP (SP standing for 'special'). Its designer, Satoru Okada, who worked on the original Game Boy, wanted to see just how thin and light he could make the GBA. The answer was very thin. By changing to a clamshell design, the GBA SP was just 80 mm square and the base was just 15 mm deep (compared with 23 mm for the GBA). This was achieved in part by installing a thin rechargeable battery, but also some electronics miniaturisation. The other major change was having a screen light. Yes – a way of seeing what you are

A Game Boy Advance SP model playing *F-14 Tomcat*.

playing when not out in the sunshine! Initially it was a front light with a button to switch it on or off below the screen. An improved backlight model (AGS-101) was available in 2005. With the light in use, the battery gave around ten hours of use, with a three-hour charge time.

Inside, the electronics and screen were pretty much the same as the GBA and it could play both old and new cartridges. Initially available only in Platinum Silver and Cobalt Blue, a full range of a dozen more colours and special editions came later.

There was much praise for the GBA SP at its launch, with just the minor criticisms of it having no headphone jack and the comment that not everyone prefers a tiny console – mainly from those with big hands!

A third and final version of the Game Boy Advance, the Game Boy Micro, was released in 2005. As its name suggests, it was even smaller than the GB SP, at just 50 mm × 101 mm × 17 mm. This in turn meant that the screen size was also reduced to a 5.1 cm diagonal, though it did have a backlight with a brightness level. The missing headphone jack from the SP was reinstated and the Micro had a removable faceplate or screen protector, which allowed for personalisation. The Micro could only play the GBA Game Paks as there was no backwards compatibility to earlier Game Boy models.

The Game Boy Micro didn't really bring anything new to the party over the SP model and, with a launch price of $99, sales were not as high as expected. This was likely due to the new Nintendo DS already being on sale before the Micro was launched. However, taken as a whole, the GBA models were incredibly successful, and by the end of 2009 over 81 million units had been sold worldwide.

The Game Boy Micro.

A Woolworths Christmas advert from the year 2000.

Nokia N-Gage (2003)

I'm sure that the N-Gage seemed like a great idea at the time. In 2003, mobile phones were really taking off and handheld games consoles such as the Game Boy Advance were selling like hot cakes. So why not combine two items into one and save both money and space in your pockets?

Finnish company Nokia were early pioneers of the mobile phone and the GSM network that connected them. After their first commercial phone, the Nokia 1011, was launched in 1992, they went from strength to strength, becoming the best-selling brand by the end of the decade. Perhaps it was the popularity of the game *Snake* on their phones that inspired Nokia to produce a phone that was also, well, sort of, a games console.

From the outside, the N-Gage looks like a strange-shaped phone, with the keypad on the right and a phone screen in the middle. But underneath, there is a slot for a memory card containing a game, although first a plastic cover and then the battery had to be removed. Play is controlled via a combination of the D-pad on the left and the keypad on the right. The screen is 5.3 cm diagonal, so not huge, and inside the N-Gage is powered by an ARM4 processor, as used on a couple of Nokia phones at the time. The N-Gage is a fully functioning phone which runs on the same Symbian operating system pioneered by Nokia that was used in their devices from 2001.

In total, fifty-eight games were released for the N-Gage, *Pathway to Glory* being Nokia's first, which received some positive reviews. However, the concept of the N-Gage just didn't work. One drawback was that the speaker and microphone were at the edge of the device, so it had to be held against the ear on its side, which felt a bit weird. Its small phone screen didn't lend itself to playing games either, nor did the phone-style buttons.

The N-Gage from Nokia.

An improved version called the N-Gage QD was released in 2004 which fixed some of the flaws. As well as having a rounder, more attractive shape, the speaker was moved to the front and the cartridge slot was made accessible without having to remove the battery.

The N-Gage was not considered a success, although by the time it was discontinued in 2006, Nokia claimed to have sold around 3 million units. With the rise of the smartphone, Nokia's once-healthy slice of the mobile phone market went into serious decline as their Symbian OS gave way to dominance from Apple's iOS and Android.

Above: N-Gage games.

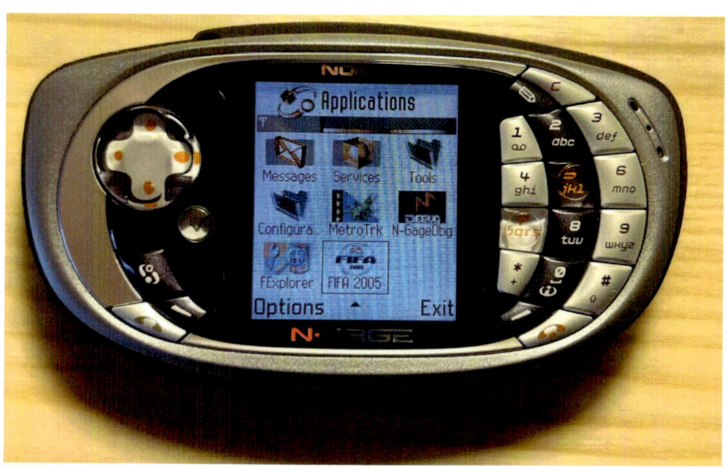

Right: The later N-Gage QD model.

Tapwave Zodiac (2003)

Personal digital assistants (PDAs) became popular in the late 1990s as tools for organising your life, and were the forerunners of today's tablets and smartphones. In 2003, a company called Tapwave went a step further and produced a PDA called Zodiac that could also play games, loaded via an SD card.

US company Palm produced the first PDAs with their widely successful Pilot range from 1996. Then, in 2001, some of Palm's former executives formed Tapwave to produce the Zodiac, which began shipping in October 2003, though UK customers had to wait another year to see them in the shops. There were two models: a Zodiac 1 with 32 MB of RAM and a Zodiac 2 with 128 MB, costing $299 and $399 respectively at launch.

At its core is a version of Palm OS, running familiar PDA applications such as a calendar, a to-do list, a graphing program called PowerOne, a word processor called Wordsmith and an eBook reader. The Zodiac could also play music via its MP3 player, display photos and play videos, though they had to be converted to its proprietary format first. Processing power is from an ARM9 processor running at 200 MHz, with access to 32 MB of RAM. To control things, there is a thumb stick and four buttons on the front, and a stylus is provided to operate the 9.7-cm touchscreen.

The Zodiac 1, showing the home screen and a skateboarding game.

It is packed with plenty of features, such as infrared and Bluetooth connectivity, stereo speakers, charging cradle, headphone jack and two SD slots, and its design put it well ahead of the pack. The tungsten-coloured aluminium case was both attractive and sturdy and gave the Zodiac the feel that this was a quality product.

Tapwave released over forty games for the Zodiac, covering the usual genres of sports, racing and arcade-style shoot 'em ups. There were also classic games such as *Hexen* and *Doom* ported to the Zodiac by enthusiasts as freeware. Any games made for Palm OS devices would also play on the device.

The Zodiac was very well received by the games industry press and praised for its high specifications. But at the time there was stiff competition from Nintendo and Sony, which ultimately forced it out of the market. By the time it was discontinued in 2005, Tapwave had sold less than 200,000 units.

Nintendo DS (2004)

The Nintendo DS was the first of the seventh generation of handheld games consoles and was seen as the successor to the Game Boy line. Its design merged the dual-screen feature of the old Game & Watch together with the clamshell of the Game Boy Advance SP and added an all-new touchscreen – their first handheld to have one and a standard feature in all future portable gaming.

It was launched in the US for $149 on 21 November 2004 to coincide with Black Friday, and sales of 1 million units by the end of the year far exceeded targets. It launched in Japan a week later, but Europe had to wait until March the following year.

As with Nintendo's previous products, the DS was available in various colours. Each country had its own specific colours, but titanium was available worldwide. Games

Nintendo's dual-screen console: the DS.

were also country-specific, with Europe having around seventeen titles at launch, including *The Urbz: Sims in the City* and *Asphalt: Urban GT*. Those games with a multiplayer mode could use the new Wi-Fi connection. The best-selling game was *New Super Mario Bros*.

Inside, it retained the ARM7TDMI processor of the Game Boy Advance (GBA) for backwards compatibility but added a second processor – an ARM946E-S running at 67 MHz. These two work together and share 4 MB of system memory. Each of the 7.6-cm screens has an uprated 2D graphics engine plus a limited amount of 3D hardware, and the lower screen (only) accepts touch input from a stylus.

There are two slots for game cards: one at the bottom edge for the older GBA cartridges and another smaller slot at the top for DS cards. This was the first portable console from Nintendo to be fitted with a rechargeable lithium-ion battery, and it gave around ten hours of use. The resulting overall package size is 14.9 cm × 8.5 cm × 2.9 cm, which is just a little bigger than the GBA.

The DS was so popular that Nintendo launched a new version in spring 2006 called the DS Lite. It wasn't light on features but was more of a slimmed-down version of the DS. Despite having a bigger-capacity battery, which gave the DS Lite at least 50 per cent greater battery life, it was 57 grams lighter than the DS. And when closed up it was only 21.5 mm thick, making it true pocket-sized. The screen brightness was increased and the screens themselves are actually 2.5 mm bigger than the DS. All in all, a package of very useful improvements.

Another new variant was released in Japan in November 2008, and April 2009 in Europe. A key feature was the ability to buy and download games from Nintendo's online store – the DSi Shop – via a Wi-Fi connection. You might therefore think that the 'i' in 'DSi' stands for 'internet', but no, it stands for 'individual'! Nintendo's home games console of the same period – the Wii – had two 'i's to represent multiplayers.

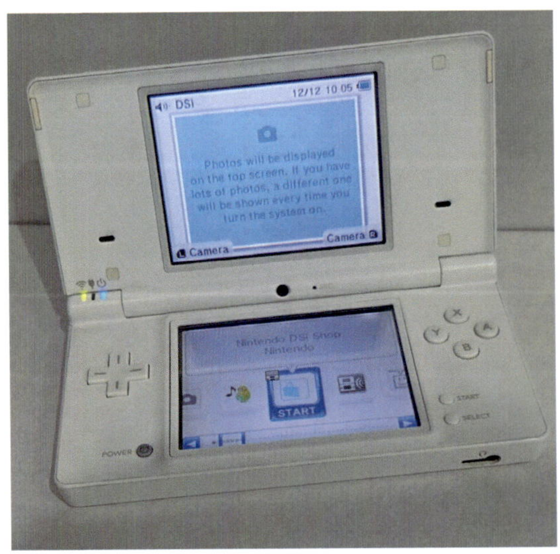

Above left: A DS Lite model playing *The Sims 3*.

Above right: The Nintendo DSi, which features a camera set into the hinge.

Another area of change was in multimedia, with voice recording and music playback. There are also two cameras – a front facing and one for selfies – and photo-editing software to, for example, add moustaches, cat ears, etc. The camera quality, at 0.3 megapixels, wasn't as good as those on mobile phones of the time, but the idea was for owners to have fun editing and sharing pictures.

The two screens were increased to 8.3 cm, making the DSi longer and wider but thinner. A necessary result of the thinning was that the old GBA slot had to go, so there was no backwards compatibility anymore. But it could still play DS games via a game card slot as well as downloading them. New games for the DSi were improved by the ARM9 processor running twice as fast as the DS and with four times the RAM.

A further variant – the DSi XL – was released a year later in November 2009. The sole purpose of this model was to supersize the gaming experience with larger 10.8-cm screens and bigger speakers. The screens also had a greater viewing angle and it was said that this would allow people surrounding the player to enjoy the game. This was the biggest and heaviest model to date and also had the greatest battery life. There were eight colours available, each with a matt interior and a glossy top surface.

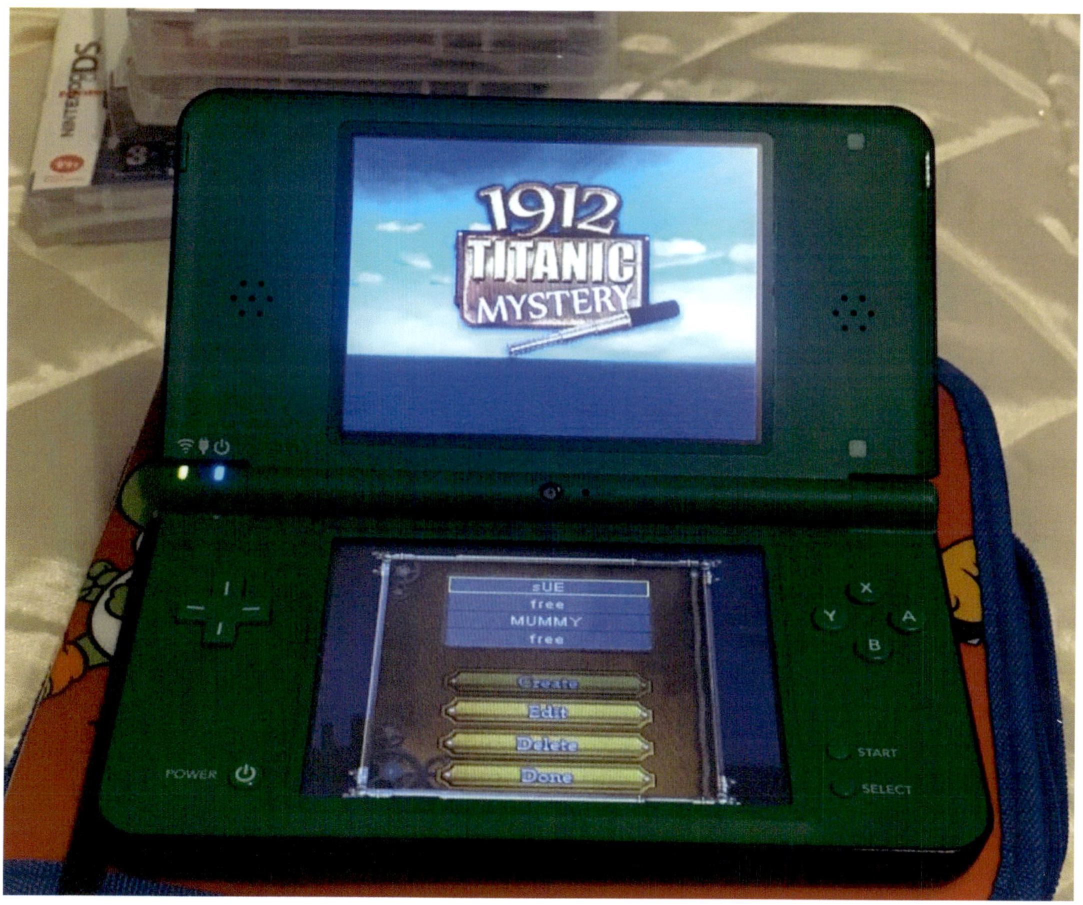

The larger Nintendo DSi XL.

The DSi sold well, with sales up to 2012 of over 40 million units. Overall, the DS range was a big success and great source of revenue for Nintendo. Combined sales of all models reached 154 million units, with the DS Lite making up the majority of those. Nintendo's only real competition during this time was from Sony's PSP.

Sony PlayStation Portable (2004)

Nintendo's DS was a slick piece of technology and, when it was released, everybody wanted one. But Nintendo could not rest on their laurels as the same year Sony brought out their first handheld: the PlayStation Portable (PSP). The PSP was packed with features, had a large screen and stylish design, and was the first handheld console in years to give Nintendo a run for their money.

Sony had launched their PlayStation range of home video game consoles ten years earlier with great success; the initial PlayStation was the first console with sales over 100 million. Sony were therefore well placed to enter the portable market. The PlayStation's games media is the optical disc, and this was replicated in the PSP which, unique for a handheld, uses the UMD (Universal Media Disc) format. These 6.4-cm discs are accessed via a read-only player in the rear, and at the time there were 1,500 movies released for the format. The image quality from the PSP's 11-cm screen with its 24-bit colour palette is particularly impressive, although, unlike the DS, it is not touch-sensitive.

A Sony PSP-1000.

The rear of the PSP, showing the disc drive cover, and some games on UMD disc.

Powering the PSP are a pair of RISC-type processors called R4000, which run at 333 MHz and have a 64-bit architecture. However, in the initial PSP model, the processors were restricted to two-thirds speed to increase the rather poor battery life. The PSP has a host of connectivity squeezed into its package size of 17 cm wide × 7.4 cm high × 2.3 cm deep, such as a USB mini-B port, a slot for a Sony's PRO-Duo flash cards, Wi-Fi and infrared, as well as a headphone jack and a serial port. In a nod to its PlayStation heritage, the PSP kept the PlayStation's signature control buttons – triangle, square, circle and cross (typically called 'ex' or 'X').

The PSP had a ten-year lifespan, during which there were 1,370 games released. Some of the most popular were *Grand Theft Auto: Liberty City Stories, Spider-Man 2, Monster Hunter Freedom Unite* and *Metal Gear Solid: Peace Walker,* which was the only PSP game to receive a perfect score from Japanese video game magazine *Famitsū.*

Though the PSP was expensive compared with the Nintendo DS, at $250, sales vastly exceeded expectations, and in the UK alone 185,000 units were sold on launch day in September 2005, doubling the record previously set by the Nintendo DS. This success inevitably led to further models in the range.

The first iteration was the PSP-2000 released in 2007. Physically, it is a few mm slimmer, which necessitated fitting a smaller battery, a strange decision as battery life was already poor. However, the old battery would still fit (without the cover) and there was now USB charging. The internal memory was doubled from 32 to 64 MB which helped with the sometimes slow loading of games from optical disc. A PSP-3000 followed in 2008, with more fairly trivial changes. The screen was now brighter, with a greater contrast ratio and faster pixel response times. Apart from a cosmetic redesign of the logos and some of the buttons, that was it.

The PSP Go model.

A more radical redesign, though, was launched in 2009 in the form of the PSP Go. The moveable screen slides upwards to reveal the game controls underneath; when in the down position, the PSP Go is a more compact device than its predecessors. In fact, with its screen size reduced to 9.6 cm, it is 35 per cent smaller than the PSP-3000. Its compactness meant that the UMD drive had to go and instead games were downloaded from the PlayStation Store. Also, the battery was non-removable. An addition, though, was Bluetooth, which allowed play from a separate controller, or a PlayStation 3. Poor sales, however, meant that it was discontinued in April 2001.

In October of the same year, Sony launched their final PSP model: the PSP Street. This was a budget version of the PSP-3000, where Sony had removed stereo sound, the microphone and Wi-Fi; all other specs, however, remained the same.

Though the PSP had a few downsides, such as cost and battery life, it was a commercial success and showed that Nintendo didn't have the handheld games market completely to themselves. In its ten-year lifespan, sales of the PSP across all models exceeded 80 million.

The PSP Street model.

OpenPandora Pandora (2010)

Even though this machine looks more like a tiny notebook computer than a games machine, its USP was that it should be an open-source design and be faster than anything currently available. It was developed from a previous machine, the GP2X from Korean company GamePark Holdings, and it was members of this GP2X community who formed the OpenPandora company to build it.

At its heart, Pandora runs a version of the Linux open-source operating system called Ångström, though users can install their own. The idea was that hobbyists and enthusiasts would write the games and also emulators for older machines such as Sega's DreamCast and Sony's PlayStation. The hardware to run them on was certainly impressive in its day.

The Pandora handheld gaming computer. (Courtesy of Michael Mrozek, CC BY 1.0)

The main processor is a 32-bit ARM Cortex-A8 running at 600 MHz, accessing 256 MB of RAM, supplemented with a PowerVR SGX530 graphics processor running at 110 MHz.

Though the case is just 14 cm × 8.4 cm × 3 cm, careful layout managed to squeeze a D-pad and game control buttons amongst the forty-three-key QWERTY keypad. Above is an 11 cm, 840 × 480 pixel screen with speakers either side. There is also Wi-Fi, Bluetooth and two SD card slots in the front. Games and software, including PDA-type applications, were downloadable from the repo.openpandora.org website.

Production was crowd funded, i.e. if you wanted one, you had to pay up front, and production only ran whilst they had enough money to sustain it. The first units were shipped in May 2010, but inevitably some customers were disappointed.

This machine wasn't about sales or competing with the big players like Nintendo and Sony, but about creating a top-end product by a community of enthusiasts in an open-source culture. A version of the Pandora was also created with a 1 GHz processor. In 2020, its successor, the Dragonbox Pyra started shipping.

Nintendo 3DS (2011)

Seeing images on a screen in true three dimensions has been a dream with film and TV makers since the dawn of the industry. The principal is that if you can send a slightly different view of an object to each eye, you will observe a stereo or 3D effect when your brain combines them. This can be achieved with a pair of glasses where a different filter over each eye (e.g. red and blue) ensures each eye only sees one of the images. Or, a clever screen can actually produce two images which are directed to each eye separately.

Nintendo jumped on the 3D bandwagon in 2011 with their Nintendo 3DS model, which creates a 3D effect without requiring any glasses. To create the two images, the screen incorporates a parallax barrier – effectively a series of vertical microscopic lenses – which direct one image to the left eye and another to the right. The effect is quite convincing, though it only works at the right distance and angle.

Apart from this novel feature, the 3DS is pretty similar to the later DS models. It has an upgraded ARM11 processor but retains the ARM9 for backwards compatibility. There is more RAM (128 GB) and an extra front-facing 0.3-megapixel camera to allow 3D photos to be taken. For gameplay, there is a new control above the D-pad called a Circle Pad which works like a thumbstick or joystick. There is also a new stylus (now extendable) to operate the lower 7.6-cm touchscreen. Although the upper screen has a much higher resolution than the DS at 800 × 240 pixels, each eye sees 400 × 240. For those that find watching in 3D a strain after a time, there is a slider by the screen to reduce or turn off the effect altogether.

There was a huge range of games produced for the 3DS in its lifetime, many but not all in 3D. The 3DS has a different shaped game card which will not fit into a DS, but DS games will play on a 3DS (minus any 3D effects).

At its launch in March 2011, the 3DS was largely well received, but a price of $250 did not encourage buyers. However, later that year, a price cut of around one-third led to a big boost in sales.

The Nintendo 3DS featured a 3D screen.

Success led to five – yes, five – more models in the range over the next six years. The first of these was a larger version, the 3DS XL, launched in Japan and Europe in July 2012. Like the DS XL, its main difference was a larger upper screen of 12.4 cm which gave a viewing area of nearly twice the size. This addressed the criticism that the 3DS was too small for adult fingers. Apart from the physical size, the only other changes are a 4-GB SD card (increased from 2 GB) and a larger battery, though this does not give any increase in battery life as the 3DS XL is more power hungry.

The next model in October 2013 was called the 2DS, and, yes, they really did remove the 3D feature. The other strange thing was that although it still had the two screens (of the sizes of the original 3DS), they changed the clamshell design to a fixed tablet-like form. The idea was that it would be a budget version of the 3DS, though, apart from lacking stereo sound, everything else was pretty much the same. This perhaps sounds like Nintendo were trying to distance themselves from 3D technology, but no, because in October the following year (2014) they released their fourth model: the New 3DS.

With the New 3DS the 3D screen was back, but this time it used face tracking via an infrared camera to improve the 3D viewing angles. There was also a faster processor and twice the amount of RAM. Visible differences on the outside are coloured X, Y, A, B buttons

The larger 3DS XL model.

The 2DS model without the hinge.

on the right and a slightly larger screen. At the same time, a New 3DS XL was launched for a little more money (£179 for the XL vs £149), with the same specs but a larger 12.4-cm screen.

A final version, the New 2DS XL, was released in 2017. This was similar to the New 3DS XL but without the 3D features, so it had the higher-spec hardware and backwards compatibly of previous models and a cheaper launch price of £129.

The New 2DS XL model.

Nintendo's experiments with 3D perhaps showed that the technology wasn't quite there yet. For every player that loved it, there was one that found it gave them eye strain. There were even concerns that it could cause harm to very young children's vision. Despite this, the 3DS range was a success and sold over 75 million units before being discontinued in 2020. The game *Mario Kart 7* was the most successful game released on the 3DS, selling around 19 million copies.

Sony PlayStation Vita (2011)

Following on from the moderate success of the PSP, in 2011 Sony decided to produce a successor, the PlayStation Vita – Vita meaning 'life'. At the time, Sony were doing well with their latest home game console, the PlayStation 3, which had been released four years earlier and had cemented Sony as a major player in the video games market. The Vita would go up against the Nintendo 3DS, but that was never going to be an easy ride.

On paper, the specs of the Vita looked promising. The large 12.7-cm screen is OLED rather than LCD, which gives a brighter, clearer image. Its touch sensitivity is also improved by using a capacitive effect rather than the older resistive-type method. Inside, there is a powerful quad-core ARM processor and a quad-core GPU from PowerVR, all contained within a single SoC. Connectivity is via Bluetooth and Wi-Fi, with games available on either PlayStation Vita game cards (flash memory) or downloadable from the PlayStation Store.

Sony's second handheld: the PlayStation Vita.

On the outside, there is a plethora of controls, including a D-pad, two joysticks, two shoulder buttons, the four PlayStation shape buttons, as well as Home, Start and Select. There are also stereo speakers and a front-facing camera.

At launch there were twenty-five games available, including *Rayman Origins* and *Fifa 12*, and there was also backwards compatibility with the PSP for digital downloads.

Initial sales in Japan and the West were strong, but declined over time, despite more game titles being made available. Whether it was due to the high price ($250) or competition from Nintendo, sales never reached the hoped-for numbers. A cheaper model, the PCH-2000, or Vita Slim, was released in 2013, which fixed some minor issues. However, its smaller screen was LCD, not OLED, and so reception was mixed. By the time the Vita was discontinued in 2019, final sales were estimated to be around 15 million, so not embarrassing, but way behind the 80 million of the 3DS.

Left: The PS Vita's OLED screen put it a cut above the competition.

Below: A later PlayStation Vita Slim.

Arduboy (2016)

Whilst the big players were spending millions on their research and development budgets and producing sophisticated games machines, we should spare a moment and look at what was available at the other end of the market.

In 2014, electronics engineer Kevin Bates designed and built his own tiny retro games machine, the Arduboy, just for fun. Originally, he had the idea of giving the gadget, which was about the size of a business card, to potential employers, but when he shared his creation on the internet the interest was so great that he left his job to work on it fulltime. A Kickstarter campaign raised over $400,000 and enabled him to produce a saleable version.

It is based on a computer board from the Arduino company, who manufacture credit-card-sized computers which run on free, open-source operating systems (typically Linux). Hobbyists and enthusiasts use them for all sorts of novel uses, such as robotics, home gadget control and software development, as they are cheap and a large online community share their resources.

The Arduboy has an 8-bit ATMega32u4 processor, 2.5 KB of RAM and 32 KB of storage. Encased in an aluminium/polycarbonate shell, it has a tiny 3.3-cm mono OLED display, six soft buttons on the front for controls, two piezo speakers and a USB port to charge the

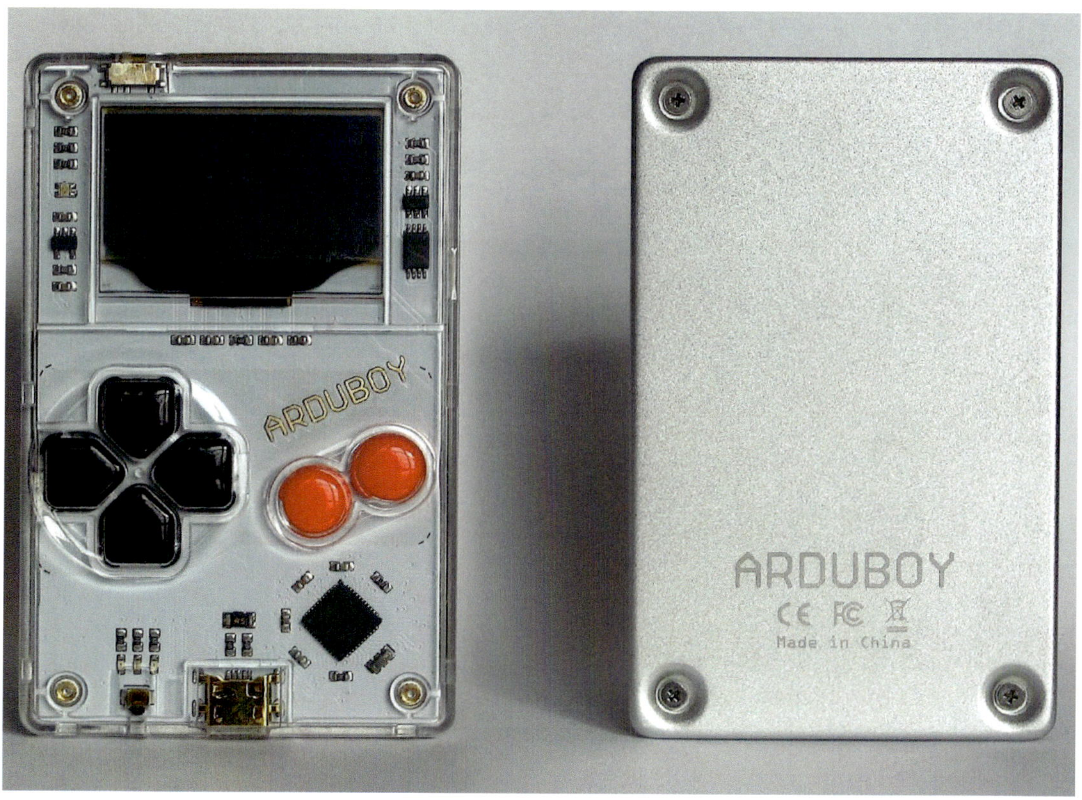

The diminutive Arduboy.

battery. Although the original design was credit card thickness, the production version, which includes proper buttons and a case, is still only 5mm thick. This was never going to be a mass-production item, but more of a 'let's see how small we can make a games computer'.

A limited number were produced, initially for $29, then $39, but the fun was either writing a game yourself or just trying out the retro games others had written. Some classic arcade games for the Arduboy are *Tank Battle*, *Block Breaker* (*Breakout*), *Alien Attack* (*Space Invaders*) and *Space Rocks* (*Asteroids*). Although they are only low-res and black and white, how else could you have as much gaming fun for the money?

Nintendo Switch (2017)

When Nintendo launched their Wii home video game console in 2006, its novel motion-sensing controllers brought a new dimension to sports games like ten-pin bowling

The distinctive-looking Nintendo Switch.

and tennis. Its successor, the Wii U, was similar, perhaps too similar, but did not get consumers buying in any great numbers. So, in 2017, Nintendo had a rethink and gave us a hybrid console: the Switch. Hybrid means that it's equally at home as a portable or as a home console connected to the TV – the best of both worlds.

To facilitate this, the left and right controllers – known as Joy-Cons – can be removed from the screen when required, e.g. when using with the TV or in multiplayer games where each player gets a Joy-Con, letting players 'switch' between the two play forms. The Joy-Cons contain motion sensors and so they can be fitted inside, say, a steering wheel accessory to give a motor sport game more realism. They can also be strapped to your wrist,

A Switch with its many accessories.

like with the Wii, for a game of tennis. As they connect to the main device via Bluetooth, they need charging periodically.

When used as a portable, you get a nice bright 15.7-cm LCD touchscreen to play on, volume controls, a game card slot on the top and rails on the side to attach the left and right Joy-Cons. For home use, the Switch comes with a docking station which allows connection to a TV via a HDMI cable for full HD-quality output.

A credible home video game console needs lots of processing power, and here the Switch doesn't disappoint. Nintendo partnered with graphics chip company Nvidia to produce a custom SoC called the Tegra X1. This beast of a chip contains no less than 256 GPU cores for graphics acceleration along with four ARM Cortex-A57 CPUs and cache memory. In technical terms, the GPU's peak performance is 393 GFLOPS (billion floating-point operations per second), which is a lot!

Like the Wii and Nintendo 3DS, games are purchased either from the online Nintendo eShop or in cartridge form, though there is no backwards compatibility with any previous console.

Following on from the Switch's success, a cheaper model – the Switch Lite – was launched in 2019 for $200. The Lite is purely a handheld model with no TV connection,

The cheaper Switch Lite.

so some Switch games that require the docking station are not compatible. This cheaper model is physically smaller, with a 14-cm screen and smaller battery; however, battery life is improved due to lower-power electronics. The Joy-Cons are fixed in place and the left one has a D-pad instead of four buttons.

Initially available in yellow, grey or turquoise, the Switch Lite was designed to fill a niche for more casual gamers that still wanted the Switch gaming experience.

A third console, the Nintendo Switch – OLED Model, was released in October 2021 as a higher-end version of the original Switch. For $350, you got an upgraded OLED screen of 17.8 cm (from 15.7 cm LCD), a metal case, more RAM and a new docking station. There were also some special editions produced such as *Super Mario Bros. Wonder*, *Pokémon Scarlet* and *Violet* and *The Legend of Zelda: Tears of the Kingdom.* Apart from that, it was pretty much as per the original Switch and fully compatible.

The Switch has been hugely popular, and as of June 2025 had sold over 153 million units across the three models, making it Nintendo's best-selling home console. The top three games – *Mario Kart 8 Deluxe*, *Animal Crossing: New Horizons* and *Super Smash Bros. Ultimate* – sold over 150 million copies between them.

Unsurprisingly, on the back of this success, Nintendo released its successor – the Switch 2 – in June 2025. There are changes throughout, including a larger 20-cm screen, more graphics processing power and memory, a new docking station and redesigned magnetic Joy-Cons. But it's still a Switch, and fully backwards compatible with its predecessor, so it will keep Switch fans happy until the next model comes along.

Blaze Evercade (2020)

For something a little bit different, the Evercade by British (yes, British!) company Blaze was all about the retro gaming experience. Blaze's first portable was the Game Gadget in 2012, which used open-source software and sold 20,000 units. Its successor, the Evercade, was designed to play authentic, authorised copies of classic arcade games by emulating the original 8- or 16-bit hardware so that the original game code could be run directly. Games are played from ROM cartridges, typically with five to twenty games on each, and a nod to the traditional method of owning physical games rather than a digital download.

Good emulation requires some serious processing power and so the Evercade uses a 1.2 GHz ARM Cortex-A7 processor with 256 MB of RAM. The screen is 10.9 cm in either a 4:3 or 16:9 ratio (switchable) with a 430 × 272-pixel resolution. There is also output to a TV via a micro-HDMI cable, giving 720p resolution.

Around eighty cartridges were produced, so hundreds of games in total. These cover arcade favourites, games from best-selling home consoles, and classic games from home computers. If you are missing *Attack of the Mutant Camels* from the Commodore 64 or *Gridrunner* from the ZX Spectrum, then get yourself an Evercade.

Though the Evercade was only produced in small numbers, it was praised for its authentic recreations of retro games and for the reasonable cost of either £60 or £80 depending on the spec. An improved Evercade EXP version was released in December 2022 with a higher screen resolution of 800 × 480, more RAM and a bigger battery.

The Evercade EXP from Blaze.

Valve Corporation Steam Deck (2022)

The Valve Corporation is an American video game developer perhaps best known for the Half-Life series, which began in 1998. They also created the hugely successful digital distribution service Steam for downloading and updating games titles, which has become the world's largest distributor of PC games. Following on from Steam's success, Valve entered the hardware market in 2015 with the Steam Machine, a small games computer running their SteamOS operating system. But in 2022 they released their first portable – the Steam Deck.

This cool-looking handheld in matt-black also runs on their SteamOS and has an impressive technical spec. The LCD screen has a 17.8 cm diagonal and a resolution of 1,280 × 800 pixels. There are no less than four CPU cores and eight GPUs, all contained within a single custom device from chip manufacturer AMD, giving a top performance of around 1.6 TFLOPs. Together with 16 GB of RAM, the specs are less than that of the typical gaming PCs that Steam's games are played on, but sufficient that the Steam Deck will play almost all of the entire Steam catalogue.

Game control is equally comprehensive with two thumbsticks, two trackpads, a directional pad, A, B, X and Y buttons, two shoulder buttons and four more on the rear. There is also haptic feedback and a built-in gyro.

Steam Decks were available with varying amount of storage, the cheapest 64 GB model costing $400 in 2022. In 2023, two OLED versions were produced with more storage, improved processors, a bigger 18.8-cm screen and improved battery life. The Steam Deck found a niche for itself playing PC games and as of 2023, 3 million units had been sold.

A Steam Deck – front and rear views.

The Steam Deck can play most games developed for the PC.

5

SMARTPHONE GAMING

Although this book is about dedicated handheld games consoles, the popularity of the smartphone as a games platform deserves a mention.

The first game on a mobile phone was *Snake*, introduced by Nokia on their 5110 in 1998. In the game, the player uses the phone's buttons to steer the snake to collect orbs which make its body grow longer. But if the snake collides with the walls or its own body, the game ends.

Since the introduction of smartphones, with their large screens and ample processing power, they have become the ideal platform for playing games on the move. Nowadays, Google's Android and Apple's iPhone completely dominate the phone market, and each has

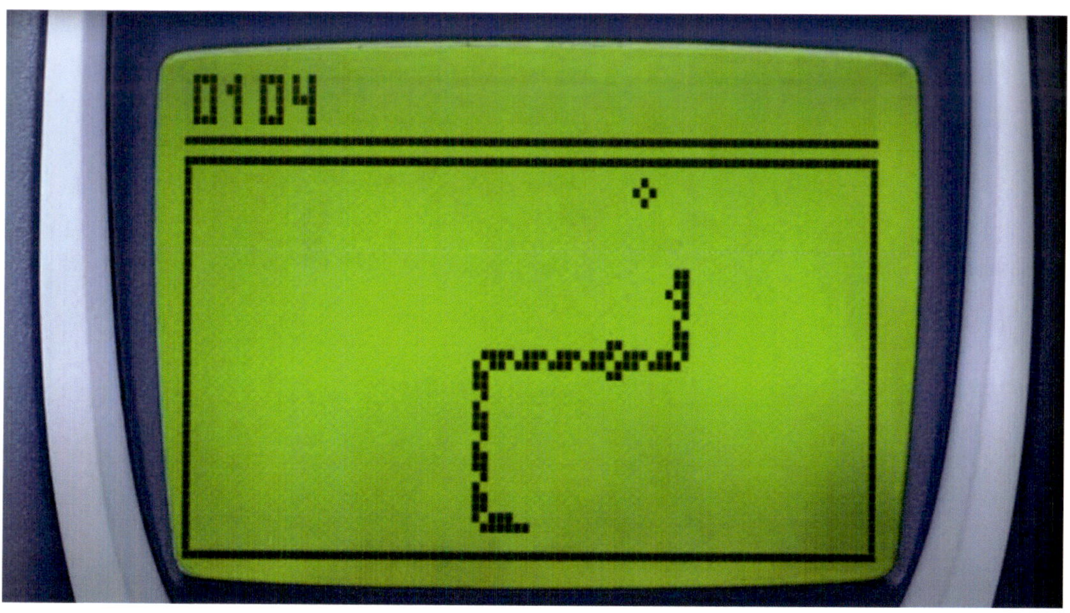

The first game on a mobile phone: *Snake*.

an app store from which games can be downloaded. Game developers make money by either charging for the download, showing adverts during play, or charging for in-game purchases. For example, *Angry Birds*, which released in 2009, originally cost $0.99, but was soon given away and showed ads to make revenue. *Candy Crush*, which released in 2012, uses the so-called 'freemium' model, where players can play for free but spend money to buy help with difficult levels. This model has generated billions of dollars in revenue for its Swedish owners, King.

One of the most successful game platforms is Roblox, where users can create their own games or choose from thousands created by others. It is mainly used by children who also use it as a social-networking platform. An example of a Roblox game is *Grow a Garden*, where you plant seeds which grow into veg, which can then be sold to earn Robux (Roblox's currency), which leads to buying some better seeds to grow more valuable veg. The game itself has pretty basic visuals, but it is quite addictive and currently has more players than *Fortnite*. In fact, by 2025, Roblox had over 83 million daily users.

The attraction of the app stores on Android and iPhone platforms is that any developer can create a game and upload it, either in the hope of making money or just for fun. You just need an idea, some software development tools, like Android Studio, and a bit of knowledge of programming and away you go.

So, smartphone gaming is here to stay, but will it replace dedicated handheld games consoles entirely? Using a smartphone as your portable gaming platform does have some drawbacks. Control is mainly just via the touchscreen, but many games benefit from a physical directional pad to give precise control over, say, your character's movements. Imagine playing *Pac-Man* without a joystick! Also, dedicated games consoles, like the Switch, currently have more graphics processing power than phones, but that gap may narrow in future.

For now, at least, portable games consoles seem to have a secure future. There is still something special about being able to carry a game with you and play it literally anywhere.

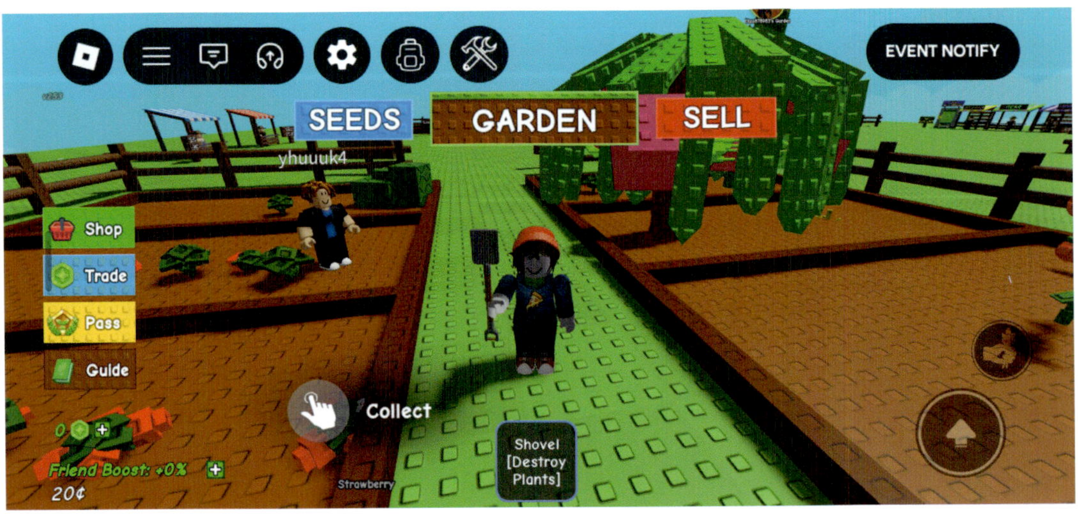

A scene from *Grow a Garden*, a Roblox game.

Above: The author's attempt at a version of *Space Invaders* for Android smartphones.

Right: The ever-popular *Candy Crush*.

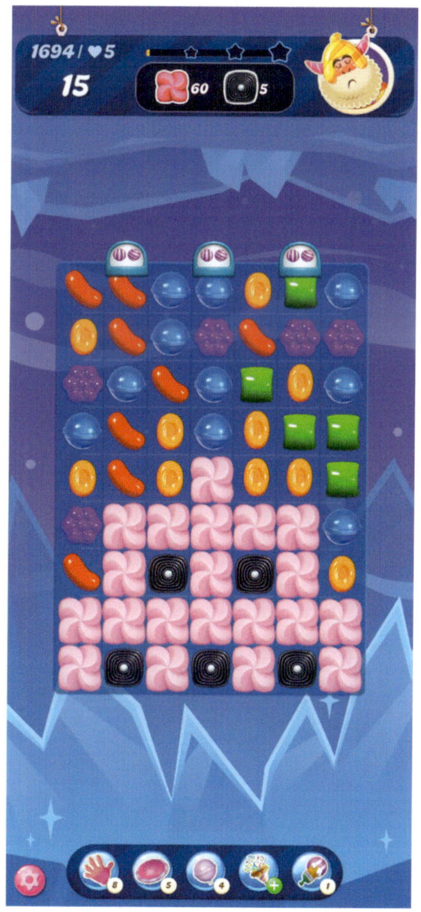

Appendix

HOW DO THEY WORK?

Handheld games consoles are (apart from the very earliest models) computers, with the same basic components as their desktop and laptop cousins. Over the decades they have become more and more sophisticated, but essentially they comprise one or more microprocessors to run the game's code, some storage memory for the code (often on a ROM cartridge), some working memory for the processor (RAM) and some video memory (RAM) for the screen.

Objects stored in the video memory (e.g. a game character) appear on the screen. The main processor's job is to run the game, including responding to user input from the controls, determining the next steps in the gameplay from, say, your character's actions, and working out where objects need to move to next. To make all this as slick as possible, the job of actually drawing objects on the screen, special effects, shadows, etc., is usually handed over to a separate graphics processing unit (GPU). There may be many GPUs working in parallel, taking workload off the main processor, making games quicker and more responsive. In computer hardware, more is usually better, so, for example, more storage in ROM or FLASH memory allows bigger, more complex games to be loaded. More RAM is then required to run these bigger games. Faster processor speeds means faster gameplay.

Early processors were 8-bit, meaning that data had to be passed around between components – for example, from memory to processor – just 8 bits, or 1 byte, at a time. When 16-bit processors came along, these sped everything up by a factor of two. Later, 32-bit highways were faster still. Processors also come with different internal architecture. Some of these, such as the ARM series, are optimised internally for speed and/or low power and so are preferred in portable consoles.

Finally, speed is also increased by packing all the electronic components as close together as possible. For this reason, the more modern consoles combine one or more processors with GPU(s) along with memory and other functions into a single device known as a system on a chip (SoC). This reduction in individual chip numbers also keeps costs down, which in turn helps sales.

The Game Boy Color motherboard showing the main components.

All good things must come to an end.

ACKNOWLEDGEMENTS

Thank you to the following resources for their invaluable information:

handheldempire.com
handheldmuseum.com